teach® yourself

**finance for
non-financial
managers**

**finance for
non-financial
managers**
philip ramsden

For UK order enquiries: please contact Bookpoint Ltd, 130 Milton Park, Abingdon, Oxon OX14 4SB. Telephone: +44 (0)1235 827720. Fax: +44 (0)1235 400454. Lines are open 09.00–18.00, Monday to Saturday, with a 24-hour message answering service. Details about our titles and how to order are available at www.teachyourself.co.uk

For USA order queries: please contact McGraw-Hill Customer Services, P.O. Box 545, Blacklick, OH 43004-0545, USA. Telephone: 1-800-722-4726. Fax: 1-614-755-5645.

For Canada order queries: please contact McGraw-Hill Ryerson Ltd, 300 Water St, Whitby, Ontario L1N 9B6, Canada. Telephone: 905 430 5000. Fax: 905 430 5020.

Long renowned as the authoritative source for self-guided learning – with more than 30 million copies sold worldwide – the *Teach Yourself* series includes over 300 titles in the fields of languages, crafts, hobbies, business and education.

British Library Cataloguing in Publication Data
A catalogue entry for this title is available from The British Library.

Library of Congress Catalog Card Number: on file

First published in UK 1996 by Hodder Headline Ltd, 338 Euston Road, London, NW1 3BH.

First published in US 1996 by Contemporary Books, a Division of the McGraw Hill Companies, 1 Prudential Plaza, 130 East Randolph Street, Chicago IL 60601 USA.

The 'Teach Yourself' name and logo are registered trade marks of Hodder & Stoughton Ltd.

This edition published 2003.

Copyright © 1996, 2003 Philip Ramsden

Typeset by Transet Limited, Coventry, England.
Printed in Great Britain for Hodder & Stoughton Educational, a division of Hodder Headline Ltd, 338 Euston Road, London NW1 3BH by Cox & Wyman Ltd, Reading, Berkshire.

Hodder Headline's policy is to use papers that are natural, renewable and recyclable products and made from wood grown in sustainable forests. The logging and manufacturing processes are expected to conform to the environmental regulations of the country of origin.

| Impression number | 10 9 8 7 6 5 4 3 |
| Year | 2008 2007 2006 2005 2004 |

contents

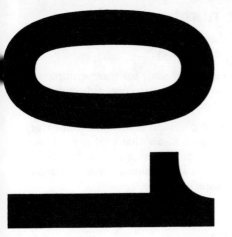

01

the purpose of accounting

In this chapter you will learn
- how accounting evolved
- about the need to record transactions
- about the need to audit this record
- how this established the basic principles of accounting

Business means numbers

If you were asked to name the principal objective of a company, would you say that it is to make money?

It's a common reply to the question and, for most companies, probably it is the main reason for their existence, although there are, of course, those organizations that are non-profit making.

One thing all businesses have in common is the need to measure that profit, or surplus, in order to know that they are, in fact, making one. But profit arises from making hundreds, thousands, even millions of business transactions – buying, selling, moving, packing, storing . . .

Recording results

So to be able to measure the profits, these transactions have to be recorded, if they have a money value. What use is a salesperson who when asked 'How much did you sell that Jaguar for?' gives the answer 'I don't know, but I did manage to sell it.'? You wouldn't know if a profit had been made on the deal, the sum to be collected from the customer, whether it would be enough to pay the manufacturer, or what the salesperson's commission (or termination payment) should be.

Paper transactions

In the business world, the language is money. But just because transactions and results are measured in Dollars or Pounds or Euros or Yen, notes and coins do not necessarily change hands every time a transaction is made. It would slow commercial activity to a snail's pace if we all had to pay as we go, so the business world operates largely on credit – take these goods now and pay me in thirty days please. But the transaction needs to be recorded, to remind the customer to pay, and you to ask him if he doesn't.

It becomes more complicated because, when you sell a product, not only do you need to remember to ask for the money later, you must also deduct the product from your stock records. Otherwise you (or your computer) might think you've still got it and try to sell it again.

There's a lot going on

Such is the volume of transactions in modern companies that whole departments are needed to handle them. Usually, Sales Order Processing administers the orders from customers served by sales representatives out in the field. Production schedulers shuffle alternatives to get sufficient product into stock to meet delivery deadlines. Buyers co-ordinate purchases and deliveries between production requirements and suppliers' lead times. And back in the offices, the Accounts department keeps track of the financial implications of all that goes on elsewhere.

What's in a name?

What is the difference between an Accounts department and a Finance department? Nothing, it's just that some companies like to call it Accounts, and others prefer Finance. There is no real distinction, although in some companies, the department may perform some duties not found in other companies, or that fall under another area. For instance, the computer section – which has other names such as IT (Information Technology) or DP (Data Processing) – may be a department on its own; it might report to the Finance Director or to the Production Director; or it may even be external to the company, a contracted-in bureau service. All in all, Accounts is Finance and vice versa.

The birth of accounting

When businesses were literally one-man operations, and the owner did all the selling and buying, he also kept his own records – how much he paid for his bushels, what he had sold them for, how many he had left at the end of the day.

Two changes in the commercial world meant things could not go on that way. First, enterprises started getting bigger, so that one person couldn't do everything. The owner needed partners or employees, although she could still take a dominant role in the proceedings. But it meant some tasks had to be delegated, and who wants to get stuck with the administration when they can give it to someone else?

Having a partner meant having to share the profits of the business, so the first step was to work out what those profits were. It hadn't been as important when Giovanni Peluga was the sole participator of his Florentine market stall – he could tell by the cash in his pocket whether he was doing all right or not. But when he had to divide it up with his partner Luigi Constantino, he wanted to be sure he was getting his fair share. So a methodology was needed to work out what that would be.

Originally, no doubt, the mathematics of the calculation of the profit was fairly simple:

'How much have you got, Giovanni?'

'Two thousand, Luigi.'

'A thousand each them.'

'Not quite, Luigi, old friend. I paid for those two hams we still haven't sold. I gave Signor Capella 150 each for them.'

'Fine, a stock adjustment – give me 850 then.'

'Wait a minute, you know those cheeses I sold to Signora Rosa, she hasn't paid for them yet. She'll give me 90 for them tomorrow.'

'I see. But did you pay Signor Grimaldi for the cheeses in the first place?'

'Only 40, on account. We still owe him another 20. And Signora Blanca brought back a loaf from yesterday, it had gone a little mouldy on the inside. I gave her a fresh one to replace it.'

'So, Giovanni, how much money can I have?'

'I don't know, Luigi, it gets more complicated every day. But I heard about this book that's come out which explains how we can work it out. It's by someone called Luca Pacioli.'

The definitive work

The book referred to by Giovanni was published in 1495 and was a treatise on mathematics and associated subjects by the Franciscan monk Luca Pacioli.

In international circles, Pacioli has two claims to fame. The first is that he collaborated with Leonardo da Vinci on a number of projects, being considered a man of high intellect himself. Secondly, his work *Summa de arithmetica, geometria proportioni et proportionalita* (to use its short name) formed the basis of accounting rules that are the underlying foundation of current finance techniques.

This is not to say that Pacioli invented accountancy or that the subject has not changed over the last five hundred years. Pacioli himself wrote in the book that the rules he was putting forward were considered best practice of the traders in northern Italy, particularly in Florence where he was based at the time. His work was the first recording in considerable detail of the principles of bookkeeping.

These basic principles, still intact in modern accounting, are as follows:
- that all transactions should be recorded in great detail in a book called the *memorandum*;
- the transactions should then be transferred to another book, the *ledger*, and that each transaction has at least two entries to it, a debit and a credit, hence the term 'double entry bookkeeping'.

There's nothing difficult about writing things down and then writing them down somewhere else in a different order, but accountants appear to have turned a simple task into a black art in the eyes of many managers from other disciplines and functions!

Accounting grows up

The second big impact on commerce came when enterprises started to get so big that they needed capital from outside investors. With managers running the company, a distinction developed between owners and managers. This separation is normal for the plcs of today but, when it first became common, the owners had to rely on reports from the management to let them know how their company was performing. They still do.

Now suppose, back in the early part of the twentieth century, you had just invested £10,000 in a textile mill operation. Three months go by and you want to know how the business is doing.

'We're doing very well indeed, sir, very well. Sales are grand, labour costs are a bit on the high side and of course the cost of cotton is going up. We'll make a nice profit this year, not much mind, because we'll need to put some on one side for one of them new steam-powered winding machines. I'll make sure you get a nice little dividend at the end of the year though, don't you worry. Besides all that, do you like my new car?'

When the year-end reports come from the mill manager, they back up what he's been saying throughout the year and you get your nice little dividend, as promised. Leaving the meeting when all the figures were announced, you notice the manager has replaced his car with another new one, the latest sporty number.

Suspicious? Why should you be? The reports from the manager confirm everything he's told you. But you've no doubt spotted the flaw – he prepares the reports!

Investors thought they needed protecting from unscrupulous managers: at best they may be hiding poor performance; at worst they may be acting fraudulently and stealing from the company (and therefore from the investors). Several notorious cases only confirmed the urgent need to introduce an independent check that would instil investor confidence. This type of check is called an audit.

The greater need for more knowledge

Given the importance of financial awareness for managers from all disciplines, the need to be familiar with the methods, concepts and principles of the world of accounting is strong. Even armed with some basic knowledge – or perhaps only with numerous assumptions – many managers still do not believe that a profitable company can actually go bust. But it can. Some circumstances surrounding a company might, at first glance, suggest that all is well. Considered observation of the company's accounts by someone with an educated eye might suggest or reveal something different.

Key points

- Accountancy, as a profession, grew up out of the need to record and present financial data as commercial organizations became bigger and the demand for accurate information grew. The principal users of the information are the managers running the company, the owners who have invested their money in it and potential investors.

- The audit was introduced as an independent check on the management's reports, but ran into several difficulties, highlighted in recent years when some published reports proved to be embarrassingly inaccurate as the companies went bust.

- There is still a need for financial information in all businesses and the Accounts department is the place to find it. The rules by which such departments operate are largely based on a five-hundred-year-old book, although frequently a technical language is used to make accountancy seem more difficult than it really is. Translation of some of this terminology follows in the next chapter.

Chapter 1 Review Question

1 What commercial developments meant that the owners of an enterprise were no longer necessarily the managers of it?

02

basic
terminology

In this chapter you will learn
- about the three major
  reports
- about debits and credits and
  ledgers
- about prepayments and
  accruals
- about the budget and equity
- about equity and gearing
- about the reconciliation of
  accounts

Accounting jargon is much like that of any other specialist subject – it makes a quick reference to longer expressions, but is handy to use when you know what the words mean.

The accounts

In business talk, 'the accounts' imply the set of reports which shows the financial standing of the company. Specifically, there are three major reports:

1 The Profit & Loss Account
2 The Balance Sheet
3 The Cash Flow Statement

Each of these is the subject of a separate chapter later.

In a less formal discussion, the accounts refer to the system of recording and reporting the financial implications of the company's activities. The key system is the general ledger, which is composed of a number of accounts in a structure appropriate to the nature of the organization. The general ledger is the financial 'bucket' into which all the financial transactions of the company are poured.

The accounts, for those composing the general ledger, can designate different levels of reporting within the business, e.g. type of cost, department, cost centre, division. Usually an account code identifies each element uniquely, particularly if the general ledger is on a computer. For instance these types of cost may be coded as follows:

Electricity	U200
Gas	U210
Oil	U220
Water	U230

Similar types of expenditure should be grouped together under one code to make summaries easier to construct, as in the above example: all utilities expenditures start with a U, and the number part of each code is related to the others. A gap of 10 is usually used so new codes can be inserted as required.

A general ledger code may appear like this:

200/U210

meaning the electricity cost (U210) for cost centre 200 (which might stand for production), or it could look like this:

014726A3964002

Although it might not be obvious, the general ledger code always has a consistent structure. In this case it might be:

first 2 characters – company code
next 4 – division code
next 5 – profit centre
next 3 – expense type

The chart of accounts will list all valid codes for each segment of the total code.

Debits and credits

These are the nuts and bolts of accounting but, when all is said and done, they are simply the financial equivalent of plus and minus.

Financial transactions are recorded in money and 'signed' with minus for a debit or plus for a credit. For any given transaction or series of transactions, the overriding rule is that the sum of the debits must equal the sum of the credits.

This means that, mathematically, the net effect on the total accounts is nil, since total debits will equal total credits. This implies that the general ledger (where all transactions are effectively stored as debits and credits) will always sum to zero and the Balance Sheet, produced on the basis of the general ledger, must, as the name suggests, balance.

Just to give you a flavour of how debits and credits apply in practice (there will be many more examples to follow), here is the accounting for paying for a maintenance bill of £1,000, settled in cash:

Debit:	Maintenance Costs £1,000
Credit:	Cash £1,000

Generally debits indicate an expense, or adding to an asset (e.g. stock). Credits imply gains (typically sales) or increases in liabilities (e.g. trade creditors).

The balancing nature of a transaction must be emphasized, no matter how many general ledger codes it affects. For example, a single gas bill for a site might be allocated to a number of cost centres:

Production	Debit	£3,000
Administration	Debit	£500
Warehouse	Debit	£1,200
Creditors	Credit	£4,700 (gas suppliers account)

Similarly the routine invoicing of a sale could be described like this:

Debtors	Debit	£5,875
Sales	Credit	£5,000
Output VAT	Credit	£875

Ledgers

Originally this term referred to the actual books in which the transactions and the accounts were recorded. Although accounts are now usually kept on computers rather than in 16-column ledger books, the principles remain the same.

The main ledgers are:

- the *sales ledger*, sometimes called the debtors ledger, which shows how much is owed to the company by each customer; the balance on each customer's account is generated from sales made to the customer less payments received.
- the *purchase* (or creditors) *ledger*, which shows how much the company owes to its suppliers; these balances are derived from invoices from the supplier for goods or services rendered, less any payments made to the supplier.
- the *general* (or nominal) *ledger*, which contains records of the financial implications of the company's transactions. Depending upon the number and nature of transactions, they may be recorded in summary form rather than in detail, although reporting systems will hopefully allow analysis of any summarized transactions into their constituent parts.

The difficulty with detailed posting (making entries in the ledgers) is that an enquiry into what has been posted may reveal that thousands of transactions make up the total. If the accountant is looking for a transaction made in error (say the sales account reads £10,000,000 when it should be £1,000,000), she would have to wade through reams of lists in the hope of finding the offending transaction. If summary postings were made daily, she could soon identify which batch looked unusually large and use the sales system to list just that day's transactions.

The general ledger is the primary source of financial information in the preparation of the Profit & Loss Account and the Balance Sheet. How the general ledger connects with the other two principal ledgers, and everything else, is disclosed later.

Accounting period

This is a notional period for recording and reporting the financial results for a given time. The usual accounting period is one year, since limited companies are legally required to prepare and submit annual accounts to Companies House, where they become available for public inspection.

The management of the company will not, of course, want to wait a year to find out what's going on. For purposes internal to the company, the financial year is broken down into shorter accounting periods. There are usually either thirteen periods of four weeks each, or twelve periods based either on calendar months or with a repeated pattern of 4–4–5 weeks. There is no best method, just what suits the organization, but be aware that, if the company is using the 4–4–5 split, it is essential to make comparisons between periods of the same length – an increase in sales figures can look very good if there are five weeks in a particular period against four in another.

Prepayments and accruals

A prepayment is an amount paid in advance but which is not deducted from the profits of the company until the time to which it relates arrives. Insurance is a good example – if the premium for the year ahead is £20,000 and this has to be paid at the start of the year, that cost should be spread over the whole financial year. After six months, £10,000 will have been charged to the Profit & Loss Account, leaving the other £10,000 as a prepayment shown in the Balance Sheet. In this way, the cost is spread over the relevant periods.

An accrual is the opposite of a prepayment. Rent for a site may be paid three months in arrears, but that doesn't mean the first two months are free! If the payment is £7,500 a quarter, then £2,500 rent should be charged to the Profit & Loss Account each month. Until the invoice for the rent is actually received or the rent paid, this amount is an accrual. The concept of accruals is explained in more detail in Chapter 3.

Journal voucher

Most real transactions are initiated by a piece of paper. A sales invoice imparts the relevant information:
- We sold goods to Mr Jonson worth £5,000.
- Mr Jonson owes us £5,000.

So on one hand, we can increase the reported sales figure by £5,000 and, on the other, the debtors by the same amount.

Some transactions which affect the company can be more apparent than real. For instance, someone whose wages are normally charged to the Inspection department has been helping out in the warehouse. So, for this month, his manager wants that wage cost to be charged to the warehouse instead.

One way of doing this would be to change the payroll system so that all costs relating to this man are charged to the warehouse. Then when he's finished his warehouse stint, the records can be reset to charge the Inspection department in future. This is messy for short-term changes.

What would normally happen is that the payroll information would go into the general ledger, possibly by an automatic transfer (interface) on the computer. This would allocate all the wage costs against the usual departments, as held on the payroll system. To move the cost from one department to another, an Accounts person with the proper authority would 'enter a journal'. This apparent sleight of hand involves no more than filling out a form (a journal voucher) showing which parts of the general ledger are to be debited (cost increased) and which credited. Depending upon the structure of the general ledger, each department has its own code and the journal is merely the transfer of amounts between places in the general ledger.

Please note that doing this does not reduce the overall wage cost to the company, it merely transfers a cost from one department to another!

Budget

The budget is a plan of what the management hope or expect the company to achieve. It normally covers a financial year, broken down into shorter accounting periods. Actual results are reported against the budget to allow the management to measure the company's progress.

The budget does not contain only financial figures, but can also include sales and production volumes to whatever level of detail (product and/or customer) management consider appropriate.

Gearing

This is an excellent price of jargon to use, because it sounds much more complicated than it is!

It is simply a comparison of the company's debt (borrowings) and its equity, to determine who's really financing the company's operations – the shareholders or the bank.

The equity is deemed to be the amount representing the shareholders' (owners') financial interests in the business. It includes the capital (the initial amount invested in setting up the company plus the proceeds of subsequent share issues), added to the retained profits of the company dating back to its first year. The shareholders extract payment from the company by way of dividends.

Although there are a number of different formulae to express a gearing ratio, they are all based around the principle of comparing the level of debt to that of equity. Or, in plainer English, it is the number you come up with when you divide the loans and preference share capital by the ordinary share capital (which is the shareholders' stake).

There is no correct figure of gearing for a company to have. It depends on the type of industry in which the company operates, the state of the industry, the company's strategic plans, its short-term requirements and all sorts of things. However, the City (meaning mostly institutional investors and their advisers) get nervous if a company has a high gearing ratio. This usually means that there is a lot of interest to be paid on loans, so less profit will be made and lower dividends go to the shareholders. On the plus side for a high gearing, it means that the shareholders aren't having to finance everything themselves and borrowed money can be used to create a higher return than it costs to borrow it.

If the gearing figure is more than 60%, it is generally regarded as high; above 100% is very high. Less than 20% could be taken as low, but in all cases it depends upon the prevailing circumstances at the time and what the point of comparison is.

Variations to the calculation include adding reserves to the ordinary share capital number or using market values instead of historic costs for the debts and the equity. (All these are fully explained when we look at the Balance Sheet in Chapter 5.) Perhaps the choice of method depends on which way whoever is calculating the gearing wants the numbers to come out!

Audit trail

This simply allows anyone, including auditors, to trace the source of any reported transaction. It is used as a check on the security and integrity of the reporting systems, to make sure that they include all transactions in the period and that no extraneous ones have crept in.

So a payment to a supplier should be capable of being traced back to the cash book and the bank statement, and should be supported by an invoice, proof of delivery of the goods and possibly even a purchase order.

Reconciliation of accounts

This refers to the check that is made on the integrity of different parts of the system. The main recording and reporting system is the general ledger, but the initial transactions are often recorded first in other ledgers and systems, principally the sales and purchase ledgers.

There will exist in the general ledger two accounts: the sales ledger control account and the purchase ledger control account. If the balances of these agree with the balances of the debtors and creditors ledger respectively, then all is in harmony.

The sales ledger has separate accounts for each customer, each of those being made up of that customer's invoices less credits notes and payments received. It is the total of all these accounts which should be represented in the sales ledger control account in the general ledger. The principle also applies to the purchase ledger.

Other reconciliations include balancing:
- the cash book to the bank statement
- general ledger payroll accounts to the payroll figures
- other debtors and creditors, such as rates and insurance which may be prepayments or accruals.

There are other phrases (plenty of them) to come, explained when they arise as we examine accounting concepts and principles, then move on to the main accounting reports.

Chapter 2 Review Questions

1 What are the three main financial reports in the 'accounts'?
2 What do debit and credit represent?
3 What is a ledger?
4 Name the three principal ledgers.
5 What is an accounting period?
6 What are prepayments? How do accruals differ from them?
7 What is a journal?
8 Define gearing.
9 What term describes the ability to trace a transaction back to its source?
10 What procedure ensures that different ledgers report the same results?

03

accounting concepts and principles

In this chapter you will learn
- about double entry bookkeeping
- about cash and accruals
- about historic cost
- about profit and cash
- about stock accounting

Accountants do have principles!

Double entry bookkeeping

The foundation of accounting and finance is double entry bookkeeping. The underlying principle is that all recorded transactions must affect at least two, but possibly more, accounts. As mentioned in Chapter 1, this is an old concept, but it has not been radically altered over the last five hundred years. By following the practices recommended by Luca Pacioli all those years ago, accountants can still ensure that their Balance Sheets always balance.

Every transaction has two or more entries in the general ledger. Here's an example based on buying stock. The debit and credit entries are abbreviated to dr and cr. The stock is bought for £1,000 on 30 days' credit and the first transaction would read:

	Dr	**Cr**	**(meaning)**
Stock	£1,000		(we have the stock)
Creditors		£1,000	(we owe someone for it)

And when the bill is paid the transaction would read:

	Dr	**Cr**	**(meaning)**
Creditors	£1,000		(pay what is owed so that the creditors' balance becomes nil)
Cash		£1,000	(reduce the cash balance)

It is only slightly more complicated if the supplier is registered for VAT (as most are) and, therefore, is obliged to add the tax to the charges at the rate of 17.5%:

	Dr	**Cr**	**(meaning)**
Stock	£1,000		
Input VAT	£175		(reclaimable from HM Customs and Excise)
Creditors		£1,175	

This is a transaction with three accounting entries, but you will notice that, as always, the entries do balance – the sum of the debits equals the sum of the credits, in this case, £1,175.

When the bill is paid, the entries look like this:

	Dr	Cr
Creditors	£1,175	
Cash		£1,175

The VAT account will be cleared when the VAT is settled at the end of the VAT period, which is usually either monthly or quarterly.

Note that the previous example concerned accounts in the Balance Sheet, since the company has not yet done anything to create a profit or loss. It has merely swapped one asset (cash) for another (stock). Now consider the selling side – £900 worth of stock sells for £1,600 plus VAT, which at 17.5% adds a further £280 to the invoice.

The transaction is described in two parts. First deal with the customer:

	Dr	Cr	(meaning)
Debtors	£1,880		(how much we are owed)
Sales		£1,600	(in the Profit and Loss Account)
Output VAT		£280	(due to HM Customs and Excise)

And now with the stock used:

	Dr	Cr	(meaning)
Cost of sales	£900		(in the Profit and Loss Account)
Stock		£900	(reduce the stock balance)

Just as a brief aside, traditionally the debit transactions are shown first, but it doesn't make any difference really.

Taking the two previous examples together (using the VAT-rated supplier of the stock and before the supplier is paid or the customer pays up), a set of accounts can be drawn up. This is based on the total entries to each account (stock, sales, etc.) that have been made and the final balance that results from the sum of all the transactions. So for instance, the general ledger for the stock account will look like this:

	Stock	
	Dr	**Cr**
Purchase	£1,000	
Sold		£900

The transaction leaves a closing balance on the stock account of £100.

In addition, you would normally also see the dates of the transactions and other relevant details, such as who the supplier and customer were and which products were bought and sold. As far as accounts are concerned it is not usually practical to keep a stock account for each product line – there could be thousands of them. That level of detail is found in the stock control system. All the accounts usually show the total value of stock, perhaps with a split between raw materials, work in progress and finished goods.

Anyway, back to our example and the complete accounts based on the two transactions we've had so far.

Profit and Loss Account

	£
Sales	1,600
Cost of sales	900
Profit	700

Balance Sheet

	£
Stock	100
Debtors	1,880
Creditors	(1,175)
VAT due	(105) (= 175 – 280)
Cash	–
Net Assets	700
Current profit	700

The Balance Sheet balances, as it must always do. Note in particular:

- The debit/credit balance of each account is not stated in the formal presentation of the results.
- The debit and credits are inferred in the Profit and Loss Account rather than specified, although sometimes the sales, or indeed the cost of sales, can be shown in brackets to identify that debits and credits have different signs.
- The current profit in the Balance Sheet is the direct link to the profit figure from the Profit and Loss Account.
- In the Balance Sheet, the use of brackets to represent credit balances is more common. However, since debtors is invariably a debit balance and creditors a credit one, brackets are often omitted and left to the assumed knowledge of the reader!

Here's a quick look at what happens when the customer pays the £1,880 and the company settles with its supplier by way of a payment of £1,175 – or if you feel you've got the hang of this, try to construct the balance sheet yourself.

Profit and Loss Account

	£
Sales	1,600
Cost of sales	900
Profit	700

Balance Sheet

	£	
Stock	100	
Debtors	–	
Creditors	–	
VAT due	(105)	(= 175 – 280)
Cash	705	(= 1,880 –1,175)
Net Assets	700	
Current profit	700	

Cash, debtors and creditors all change, but the Balance Sheet still balances!

Note that the Profit and Loss Account doesn't change at all when payments are made or received, because nothing has happened which would create a profit or a loss – assets and liabilities have only changed form (debtors to cash received, creditors to cash paid). Cash is not the same as profit, a point which will be emphasized shortly.

In double entry bookkeeping, if you make sure that each individual transaction balances (all the debits equal all the credits), no matter how complicated the transactions might appear, and no matter how many of them there are, in the end the Balance Sheet must balance too.

Cash v. accruals

Possibly, the most important concept in accounting is the distinction between cash transactions and 'accruals'. Put in accounting parlance, the accrual concept matches the transaction to the accounting period in which it occurs, not when cash payment is subsequently made or received.

In plainer English, accountants want to reflect in their accounts for a particular accounting period all the things that happened during that period, without waiting for the resulting cash side of things to catch up.

Consider the previous purchase of stock, excluding the VAT to start with. The stock is acquired in January, but on 60 days' credit terms. So payment is not due until March. Even so, we want to recognize that the purchase has been incurred in January and so it is included in January's accounts. We can't pretend that, just because we don't have to pay for the goods until March, we didn't have them until then.

Hence the transactions recorded in the ledgers are:

January		March	
	£		£
Stock	**Dr** 1,000	**Creditors**	**Dr** 1,000
Creditors	**Cr** 1,000	**Cash**	**Cr** 1,000

Normally a supplier would submit a purchase invoice for the goods when the items are delivered, or very soon afterwards. This is usually the document that triggers the recognition that a financial transaction has been incurred.

However, if the supplier does not actually send an invoice along with the goods or by the time the entries for the accounting period are closed, it does not mean that the organization can pretend that the stock either never arrived or was free. Instead of putting the credit entry into the creditors account, a more general one called 'goods received not invoiced' (GRNI) is used. The GRNI account would appear in the current liabilities section of the Balance Sheet, close to the creditors, since it represents much the same thing – it's what the company owes someone for goods or services provided.

Depending upon the control systems that the company has in place for monitoring such activities, it is likely that a goods received note, filled in by the Goods Receiving or Warehouse department, would be the main document for Accounts to use for this purpose.

The key point is to recognize and reflect in the accounts all financial transactions in the accounting period in which they occur, not when the paperwork catches up.

The technical term for this is the accruals concept, as opposed to cash accounting. Small businesses (very small ones) may prefer to use cash accounting, which only recognizes transactions when they are resolved in cash – a sale is not perceived as such until the cash is received from the customer. Bear in mind this could be several months after the event took place.

So, when accountants say they will accrue for something, all they mean is that the paperwork for this transaction hasn't come through for it yet, but they will make an adjustment to the accounts *as if it had*.

The adjustment is made by way of a journal voucher posted to the general ledger.

Historic cost

All the figures in accounts are prepared based on historic cost, which simply means the cost of the thing at the time it was incurred. Normally this is not a particular problem – if a sale was made in January of 10 tonnes of lead at £400 a tonne, then the sales and debtors accounts show £4,000, even if the price of lead moves to £500 in February (lead is a commodity with a fluctuating price). Figures are not restated, but kept at what they were when the transaction took place.

There are two possible exceptions to this.

1 Stock is valued at the lower of cost or net realizable value. Invariably, this leads to stock being valued at cost – what the organization paid for it at the time it acquired it – because the intention is to sell the stock at more than it cost. However, changing market circumstances may mean that this is impossible (the product may be obsolete or perhaps be a market commodity whose price had fallen). On such occasions, it is deemed prudent to revalue the stock at how much it *could* be sold for – the net realizable cost. 'Net' simply means after the transport or handling charges needed to dispose of the stock.

   However, because of the nature of most items held in stock and the way in which stock is sold, it can occasionally be revalued. When stock is valued at standard cost (a benchmark cost given to a stock item – see Chapter 11), this occurs usually annually, if not more often. Revaluation will occur when actual costs, that the company is paying out to suppliers, have changed significantly from the standard costs used to value the stock. Standard costing is investigated in more detail in Chapter 11.

2 The other exception is to do with fixed assets and we have already referred to this point.

Imagine that a company purchased its headquarters 30 years ago for £100,000. If the building were to be depreciated over 50 years, the current net book value (the original cost less accumulated depreciation) of the building in the accounts would be £40,000 (depreciation is calculated at £2,000 a year for 30 years = £60,000, deducted from the original cost to give the net book value). Depending upon its location, the building is not only likely to be worth more than that if sold, but even more than was paid for it in the first place. This leads to the obvious conclusion that accounts ignore inflation – they do. Attempts have been made to replace historic cost accounting with current cost accounting, but generally these have created more problems than they have solved.

Back to the building which, following depreciation, has been accounted for 'in the books' at just £40,000. It is permissible for the directors, with the advice of professionals (usually chartered surveyors), to revalue the fixed assets in the accounts. Assume these fine headquarters could now fetch £500,000 if sold. Does that mean the organization can add a windfall £460,000 to its profits for the year?

The accounts have to be made to balance. If fixed assets are to be restated upwards by £460,000, what is the other entry? The answer is the creation of a revaluation reserve in the equity part of the Balance Sheet, rather than adding to the current profitability of the company. The sensible logic behind this is that the apparent gain is only a notional one until the building is actually sold. It would be foolish to pretend that an organization is making healthy profits when all it is doing is occupying a building whose value increases every year. As a safeguard, there is a legal prevention from distributing the revaluation reserve as part of the dividend payment to the shareholders, since it is not a real profit.

So why revalue fixed assets? Only to reflect more accurately the value of the assets of the company as stated in the balance sheet.

The alternative to using the historic cost convention presents a great dilemma to the accountancy world. The problem arises from the fact that historic costs do not, by definition, reflect the real, up-to-date, intrinsic value of the assets on a company's Balance Sheet. Thus, if investors and potential investors (including other companies who might want to take it over) use the accounts to form the basis of their investment strategy, they might not get an accurate picture of the true worth of the company's assets.

Statement of Standard Accounting Practice, number 16, recommended that various figures in the Balance Sheet should be restated at replacement cost values, but this was eventually withdrawn after much controversy.

The main figures that would be affected by such a rule are the stock and the fixed assets. Debtors and creditors wouldn't change – if a customer owes £8,000, all you'll ever get is £8,000, no matter when he pays. On the other hand, stock may cost more to replace now than when it was bought, since prices tend to rise rather than fall. Revaluing the stock at replacement cost rather than historic increases the asset value of the company and, to make the whole thing balance, the profits must rise by the same amount. Of course, in reality, nothing has happened. The same quantity of stock is still there, so this is merely a paper increase in value, a trick of accountancy. It is easy to see why it fell into disrepute.

No alternative method has yet been proposed successfully.

Profit v. cash

Although we have already discussed the accruals concept – that the accounts reflect activities which have occurred and not just those backed by the exchange of cash – it is important to stress the difference between profit and cash.

It is perfectly feasible for a company to go bust while it is making profits. Indeed, this is the most common cause of failure among start-up businesses. An example will show why. Consider the first few months of trading for Aardvark Overseas Limited, a company supplying statues of exotic animals.

	Jan	Feb	Mar	Apr	May
Sales (£)	5,000	7,000	10,000	15,000	18,000
Purchases (£)	7,000	8,000	6,000	10,000	10,000
Overheads (£)	2,000	2,000	2,000	2,000	2,000

Obviously, the company has some stock left at the end of each month, but first let's calculate the profit, assuming that the company makes a gross margin of 40% on its sales (which is the same as saying the cost of sales is 60% of the sales value).

So in January, sales are £5,000. Therefore, the cost of sales is 60% × £5,000 = £3,000, leaving a gross margin of £2,000. Then the closing stock for January is worked out by:

Opening stock	–
Purchases (£)	7,000
Cost of sales (COS) (£)	(3,000)
Closing stock (£)	4,000

That is: what we started with

plus: what was bought

less: what was used

giving: what's left.

The stock position for all the months looks like this:

	Jan	Feb	Mar	Apr	May
Opening (£)	–	4,000	7,800	7,800	8,800
Purchases (£)	7,000	8,000	6,000	10,000	10,000
COS (£)	(3,000)	(4,200)	(6,000)	(9,000)	(10,800)
Closing (£)	4,000	7,800	7,800	8,800	8,000

(Note that the closing stock for one month becomes the opening stock for the next and that the cost of sales in each month is 60% of sales.)

We can now put together a Profit and Loss Account:

	Jan	Feb	Mar	Apr	May
Sales (£)	5,000	7,000	10,000	15,000	18,000
COS (£)	(3,000)	(4,200)	(6,000)	(9,000)	(10,800)
Gross margin (£)	2,000	2,800	4,000	6,000	7,200
Overheads (£)	(2,000)	(2,000)	(2,000)	(2,000)	(2,000)
Profit (£)	–	800	2,000	4,000	5,200

That's a total of £12,000 profit in five months and improving all the time after a slow start.

Let us suppose, however, that because this is a new business venture, the company finds it difficult to get credit for its supplies, since it has no track record for paying out. It has to pay its suppliers the following month after the goods are received, but all overheads (salaries, rent etc.) are paid in the month in which they are incurred.

Also, to attract customers, it offers to give them credit of three months, so sales in January are paid for in April.

Assuming the company started off with £10,000 in cash (from the shareholders), the cash flow looks like this:

	Jan	Feb	Mar	Apr	May
Opening (£)	10,000	8,000	(1,000)	(11,000)	(14,000)
Receipts (£)	–	–	–	5,000	7,000
Payments:					
Suppliers (£)	–	(7,000)	(8,000)	(6,000)	(10,000)
Overheads (£)	(2,000)	(2,000)	(2,000)	(2,000)	(2,000)
Closing (£)	8,000	(1,000)	(11,000)	(14,000)	(19,000)

(Note that April's receipts are from sales in January. Payments to suppliers in February are from January's purchases.)

Thereafter, the cash position improves (feel free to extend the cash flow yourself), but at the worst point, the company needs to find another source of funding for £19,000. A simple bank overdraft may do it, but there may not be a bank willing to lend to what may seem a risky enterprise. Yet all the time, the company is profitable. So a profit does not automatically mean a cash surplus.

It is a lack of cash and the resulting inability to finance its operations that leads to the downfall of many companies, rather than a lack of profit. Just imagine how much worse it would have been if the company had been making losses during its first few months, while it became established!

Accounting for stock

You would think that stock is stock is stock and working out its value is fairly simple – it's what you paid for it (unless you're using standard costing).

Consider the following sequence of transactions when stock is bought and sold. Let's say this company deals in the distribution of cans of soft drinks and this is what happens to just one of the product lines:

1 March	buy 1,000 cans at 8p each
12 March	buy 2,000 cans at 7p each
15 March	sell 1,200 cans for 14p each
17 March	buy 1,000 cans at 9p each
22 March	sell 2,200 cans at 12p each

From the above, the sales revenue is £432 (1,200 at 14p plus 2,200 at 12p). Overall the company has bought 4,000 cans for a total of £310. There are 600 cans left in stock at the end of March.

What is the stock value at the end of March? Is it:

a £54
b £48
c £47.57?

The maths of the matter is quite simple – there were three receipts into stock at varying prices. How much they were sold for does not affect the stock value or the cost of sales calculation.

So the right answer is – all of them, depending upon the method used to account for stock. There are three methods (hence the three answers!) and they are all perfectly acceptable.

1 First in first out (FIFO)

The assumption is that the stock which is received first is also the first that is used. This leads to the following calculation of stock, using the above transactions (sales shown in brackets):

Date	Quantity	Cost each	Balance Value (£)	Quantity	Value (£)
1 March	1,000	8p	80	1,000	80
12 March	2,000	7p	140	3,000	220
15 March	(1,000)	8p	(80)		
	(200)	7p	(14)		
Total	(1,200)		(94)	1,800	126

17 March	1,000	9p	90	2,800	216
22 March	(1,800)	7p	(126)		
	(400)	9p	(36)		
Total	(2,200)		(162)	600	54

For the sale of 1,200 cans made on 15 March, the first 1,000 are deemed to have come from the batch bought on 1 March and the balance from the batch bought on 12 March. Similarly for the 2,200 sold on the 22 March – the first 1,800 finish off the batch from 12 March and the rest come from the last batch. Each batch is costed at the price paid.

As a check, the 600 cans left in stock at the end of the month must be from the last batch bought at 9p each – and 600 at 9p is £54.

2 Last in first out (LIFO)

LIFO uses the opposite assumption to FIFO, in that the stock received last is used first. Think of the warehouseman putting the cans into a storeroom which gets fuller with every delivery. Is he going to take all the cans out to get to the ones at the back? No, he'll take the nearest ones, those he put in last.

So how does this change the calculations?

				Balance	
Date	Quantity	Cost each	Value (£)	Quantity	Value (£)
1 March	1,000	8p	80	1,000	80
12 March	2,000	7p	140	3,000	220
15 March	(1,200)	7p	(84)	1,800	136
17 March	1,000	9p	90	2,800	226
22 March	(1,000)	9p	(90)		
	(800)	7p	(56)		
	(400)	8p	(32)		
Total	(2,200)		(178)	600	48

Note that the first two lines are the same as FIFO. All of those sold on 15 March come from the last batch bought on 12 March. The 2,200 sold on 22 March is a little more complicated – the first 1,000 are those received on 17 March, another 800 completed those from 12 March and then there were 400 from the very first batch.

To confirm the value, the 600 cans left at the end of the month must be from the batch bought on 1 March at 8p each – 600 at 8p is £48.

3 Average cost

This method takes the middle ground and assumes that we don't know which end of the stock pile the Despatch department is taking things from. So we average the cost out after every transaction.

This leads to the following calculations:

Date	Quantity	Cost each	Balance Value (£)	Quantity	Value (£)
1 March	1,000	8p	80	1,000	80
12 March	2,000	7p	140	3,000	220
15 March	(1,200)	7.3p	(88)	1,000	132
17 March	1,000	9p	90	2,800	222
22 March	(2,200)	7.9p	(174.43)	600	47.57

Again the first two lines are the same as the previous examples. However, on 12 March we have 3,000 cans which cost £80 plus £140 = £220, average 7.3p each. Every time we receive more cans, the quantity and total value go up and a new average is calculated to determine the cost of sales.

In an ideal world, a company would match the accounting method to the physical operations that actually take place in the warehouse. There is no requirement that this be the case, but it is something the auditors would have an eye on: that the appropriate method is being applied. In circumstances where the stock is turned over quickly (i.e. it's not long between it being received from the supplier and it going back out again to a customer) and stock levels are fairly low, then it may not make much difference which method is used.

However, if a company uses LIFO at a time of rising prices, there is a chance that the stock is being undervalued, since the original stock values may now be quite different from current prices. FIFO is generally more up to date.

It is perhaps unnerving that, given those same transactions happening in three separate companies using different stock accounting methods, we can end up with three different stock valuations, all of which are perfectly defensible. It's just the nature of some parts of the financial world.

Finally a company may choose to change its stock valuation policy – perhaps not surprisingly, this usually leads to an increase in the value of the stock and a paper profit. (A paper profit is one that is created by accounting adjustments, rather than a real one made by the business transactions of the company. A paper profit cannot be realized in pound notes.) Any such change has to appear in a note to the published accounts and, of course, needs the tacit agreement of the auditors.

Key points

- **Double entry bookkeeping** – for any given financial transaction, the sum of the debits must always equal the sum of the credits.

- **Cash v. accruals** – accounting records the financial effect of transactions in the period in which they occur, not when they are settled in cash (the accruals concept).

- **Historic cost** – is valuing everything at the cost when it was done, not what it might be worth now. This is the basis of the figures in the financial reports, but it does mean that they could be out of date and possibly misleading.

- **Profit v. cash** – the two do not necessarily coincide. A profitable company can run out of cash by paying its creditors before being paid by its debtors.

- **Stock accounting** – three valid methods are FIFO (first in first out), LIFO (last in first out) and average cost. All three are perfectly acceptable, but give different valuations for closing stocks.

Back to the real world

Armed now with an understanding of what accountants mean when they speak of accruals and historic costs, amongst other phrases, it's time to tackle the end result of all their tinkering – the financial results, starting with the Profit and Loss Account.

Chapter 3 Review Questions

1 What is the key principle of double entry bookkeeping?

2 What does an accrual do to the accounts?

3 What is the historic cost basis?

4 Distinguish between profit and cash. Under what circumstances could a profitable company have a net reduction in cash?

5 What are the differences in the major stock valuation methods of FIFO, LIFO and average cost?

04

the profit and loss account

In this chapter you will lear
- how to understand the pr
  and loss account
- about the profit and loss
  account in management
- about 'the bottom line'

Reporting

The three major financial reports are the Profit and Loss Account, the Balance Sheet and the Cash Flow Statement.

All limited companies are required by law to produce an annual set of accounts, in a prescribed format. These will contain a Profit and Loss (P&L) Account, a Balance Sheet and a Cash Flow Statement, together with notes to the accounts which explain some of the detail behind the numbers and some further explanation of the accounting policies used to determine them.

These statutory accounts, as they are called, are available from Companies House, which has its main office in Cardiff, with other offices around the UK (see Appendix C).

A P&L Account for use by the company's management will have more detail than the one in the statutory accounts. Not only that, but the numbers can be different too! The reason is that one version of the P&L Account tells the managers how profitably they have run the company, but the one published in the statutory accounts may contain 'adjustments' which, although technically valid, give the management some leeway on what they wish to publicly report.

This is not to suggest that the published profitability is in any way false or just made up; rather, the management can take advantage of some accountancy 'tricks' to adjust the reported profit in either direction. Although we will look at some such technical adjustments in more detail later, one example is capitalisation of interest.

Say a retail company is building a new store. The cost is £10m. The finished store becomes a fixed asset in the company's accounts, at a cost of £10m. But suppose, instead of paying cash for the building, the company borrowed from the bank and paid say £2m in interest charges, what is the cost of the building now? Some companies would add that £2m to the asset value of the building. The alternative would be to reduce the profits of the company by £2m by charging the interest to the profits. So we have a building that can be valued at either £10m or £12m, but it's the same building!

This accounting adjustment would not interest the company's managers in the first instance. They would want to know what the 'real' profit is – what the company has achieved under their direction. Once that is established, they leave any further adjustments to the accountants who will try to convince the auditors of the merits of the adjustments.

So, for the moment, we will concentrate on what the management would find useful in a P&L Account. In other companies, the same report may be referred to as an income statement or an operating results statement. Broadly, these are the same thing, although the level of detail may vary.

A P&L Account format for management use may look like this:

P&L Account for the year ending 31 March 2006		
	£000s	£000s
Sales		34,252
Cost of Sales:		
Materials	10,429	
Labour	4,731	
Direct costs	3,390	
Total cost of sales		18,550
Gross profit		15,702
GP %		45.8%
Overheads:		
Staff costs	5,630	
Indirect costs	4,350	
Depreciation	1,422	
Total overheads		11,402
Profit before interest and tax		4,300
Interest:		
Receivable	112	
Payable	604	
Net interest		492
Profit before tax		3,808

For management purposes, the P&L Account is not likely to go as far as showing tax, since this is largely an area beyond management's control, being a specialist subject in its own right. That does not mean it should be ignored, because good tax planning can save companies a considerable amount of money, but professional advice is usually taken in this respect.

Also the management would expect to receive monthly reports on the company's profitability with the appropriate analysis, perhaps with a year-to-date column and a comparison against a budget or plan. The statutory accounts, by contrast, are only produced annually.

Let's consider each line in the P&L Account in detail and what it actually represents.

Sales – this is the amount, excluding VAT, invoiced to customers for goods or services rendered. The figure will normally be the full invoice amount before any allowances for discounts or early payment settlements.

For instance, we could charge Edison Lighthouses Limited £5,000 (before VAT) for products, but the terms under which we trade may offer them a 5% discount if they pay within seven days. Whether they pay in seven days and take the discount or not, the sales figure remains the same: £5,000.

The sales figure is always shown without VAT, because eventually this has to be paid over to HM Customs and Excise, so it has no effect on the company's profit.

Any discounts taken are usually charged to a Discounts line in the overheads section.

Credit notes issued to customers (for goods rejected or invoicing errors) are deducted from the sales figure, so that the net figure is shown after all credits.

Cost of sales – as it seems to indicate, this is the cost to the company of making and/or supplying the products that were invoiced to the customers. If the company does not have a standard costing system (explanation in detail will be forthcoming in Chapter 11), then it can use actual costs in the following simple manner. Depending how the costing structure of the products is set up, up to three elements are commonly found, although they are not always split in the Profit and Loss Account:

1 Working out the *cost of materials* becomes a simple mathematical exercise. Add to the opening stock (the stock value at the start of the accounting period) the value of products purchased during the period to give a subtotal of stock available for sale. Subtract from that the closing stock value (the stock value at the end of the period) and you must be left with what was used. This becomes the cost of sales. Theoretically, the figure is distorted by any stock adjustments (i.e. shrinkage or damaged stock), but they will have to be 'written off' at some point, since they would be no longer saleable.

   (NB The term 'written off', much beloved by accountants in the presence of non-financial managers, simply means that the item in question is deemed to be worth nothing, so its cost is to be written off as an expense somewhere in the P&L account, that is, deducted from profit.)

The calculation looks like this:

	Opening balance	240,212
add:	Purchases	88,609
	Available for use	328,821
less:	Closing stock	212,604
	Cost of sales	116,217 (stock used)

2 *Labour* can be taken as the actual wages incurred by the production departments in making the products for sale. Technically, there will be a timing difference between the products being made and those being sold, since the finished items go into stock first. Accountants can adjust this by allowing for increases or falls in the stock level, but if production and sales quantities are relatively similar, the timing difference is insignificant. It is permissible for part of the labour cost to be included in the valuation of the stock, so it is not deducted from the profit until that stock is sold. The logic is that it costs money to use labour to transform raw materials into work in progress and finished goods, so the value should reflect that. Direct costs can also be incorporated into the stock value, for the same reason.

3 *Direct costs* are basically production overheads, and the actual costs incurred can be used. This will include such expenses as electricity, perhaps a share of the rates bill, depreciation of factory plant and machinery. In theory if there was no production, there would be nil direct production costs, which is a pretty useful definition of what a direct production cost is. This doesn't hold for the rates charge (it's a fixed cost for the year), but most companies would include it anyway, since a factory is the major reason for the rates bill being the size that it is.

A detailed explanation of standard costs is given in Chapter 11. At this point, let it suffice to say that the cost of making a single unit of the product can be given a theoretical cost for each element of material, labour and direct overhead. The cost of sales in the P&L Account is then the sold quantity multiplied by these costs per unit. This figure can then be amended up or down by any variances in manufacturing performance between the expected standards and actual. A more complicated explanation lays ahead!

Gross Profit – is simply the difference between the sales and the cost of sales. However, it can be read as a simple measure of the profitability of making or supplying the product to customers, before taking into consideration indirect and fixed costs.

Overheads – covers costs and expenses which are not directly associated with the production of the goods, but include all the necessary support functions needed to run the company. In our example (page 36) the overheads have been broken down into staff costs, depreciation and indirect costs. There is no doubt that management would have access to a more detailed analysis of the figures that lay behind these costs. The analysis may be by department and would certainly, in the case of indirect overhead costs, go down to the level of recording the type of cost, e.g. stationery, equipment hire, legal fees, bank charges, etc.

Senior management may not want to know what the stationery bill for the period is, but somebody somewhere in the organization ought to know. Otherwise how could the cost of anything be monitored and controlled?

The staff costs will relate to the salaries/wages, pension and National Insurance contributions of the company for employees not directly related to production (i.e. those not included in the labour figure under cost of sales). So the wage costs of Sales and Marketing, Human Resources, Management, Administration, IT, R&D and even Accounts will be included.

Depreciation – this is such a commonly misunderstood term that a full explanation is merited at this point. The concept stems from how the profits should be affected if a company buys an expensive piece of capital equipment or an equally costly building. If the company's annual profits are say £8m, and a new milling machine costs £2m, how does this affect the reported profit?

The argument for using depreciation runs along these lines:
- given that the company is performing consistently, we would expect to see a consistent result in the reported profits of the company
- the milling machine will last for ten years
- to report suddenly only a £6m profit would make management appear, at first glance, to be less effective than they really had been
- so, if the machine will last for ten years, let's give a tenth of the cost of it to each of these years and reduce the profit accordingly – by £200,000 for each year, rather than by £2m in a single year.

The depreciation is the amount deducted from profits by dividing the original cost of the capital item by how long it should last (technically, its economic life).

This is called the *straight line method*. There are numerous ways of calculating the depreciation each year, but this is the most popular and it is used in all the examples in this book, with the exception of this next one.

The *reducing balance method* calculates depreciation as a percentage of the closing net book value, e.g. if the depreciation is set at 10% p.a. and the original cost was £10,000:

Original cost	£10,000
Year 1 depreciation	(£1,000)
Net book value	£9,000
Year 2 depreciation	(£900)
Net book value	£8,100
Year 3 depreciation	£810
Net book value	£7,390 and so on.

It takes longer to fully depreciate the asset than it would using the straight line method over ten years.

Note that the depreciation amount is not affected by when the item is paid for – it could be paid for by cash on delivery, 30 days' credit, a seven-year lease contract, or whatever. Cash has nothing to do with depreciation and vice versa. Depreciation is purely an accounting adjustment to spread the cost of the item over a number of years rather than take a big reduction in the profits of one year. The company does not literally put aside cash to pay for a new one when the old one is obsolete (see also *fixed assets*).

Profit before interest and tax (PBIT) – is simply a subtotal, although this is most often the line on the P&L Account which managers accept as being the best measure of their performance. Subsequent additional reductions in this profit figure, namely interest and tax, could be considered beyond the control of most of the managers involved in operational activities, so this is why they tend to think of PBIT, and sometimes refer to it, as the 'bottom line'. To be more accurate, the real 'bottom line' is literally the last line on the published P&L Account, after all deductions for interest, tax and dividends have been made, but the PBIT does for most managers.

Interest – is a common enough concept, and fortunate is the company that receives more than it pays. Such a company may have good cash management, or just be in the sort of business that encourages a build up of cash (e.g. retail outlets, which get paid in cash (or near cash) by customers, but have their supplies on credit terms).

Normally interest payable is a straightforward deduction from the profit, except in those cases where a company decides to capitalize some interest as being part of a fixed asset project that required loans to carry it out. Of course this means less interest is deducted from the profit, so the profit is higher, which is generally a nice thing for managers to see!

Note that it is the true 'bottom line' – the profit after interest, tax and dividends – which is carried over to the balance sheet as this year's profit.

The P&L Account in the statutory accounts

The statutory accounts are accessible to the public (and other companies or their accountants) via Companies House, so companies generally try to report the minimum possible. There will be far less detail in the statutory format than in the management accounts, although there will be some explanatory notes.

A typical Profit and Loss Account in the statutory accounts may look as simple as this:

Io Exploration Limited
Profit and Loss Account
for the twelve months ended 30 June 2006

	Notes	Year ended 30.06.06 £000	Year ended 30.06.05 £000
Turnover	1		
– continuing operations		892	832
Cost of sales		<u>612</u>	<u>574</u>
Gross profit		280	258
Other operating expenses	2	<u>204</u>	<u>196</u>

Profit on ordinary activities before interest	76	62
Interest payable	44	56
Profit on ordinary activities before taxation	32	6
Tax	6	1
Profit on ordinary activities after taxation	26	5

Even the explanatory notes 1 and 2 do not give a lot away – there will be details of sales by region, specific deductions from profit (such as depreciation, the audit fee and operating rentals) and perhaps, most interestingly, an indication of payments to directors. Individuals are not named specifically and the note will appear like this:

Emoluments of highest-paid director £84,200
Emoluments of other directors:

	No. of directors
£0 – £5,000	2
£50,001 – £60,000	1
£60,001 – £70,000	1

The two directors paid below £5,000 are likely to be non-executive directors, who have an advisory role rather than daily participation in the running of the company.

Key points

- There can be a difference between the profit in the published statutory accounts and that in the management accounts seen only by the company's management.
- Statutory accounts for limited companies must be filed at Companies House within nine months of the company's financial year end, after which anyone can get a copy (for a small fee).
- Management will have available detailed analysis of the figures in the Profit and Loss Account, including a breakdown of sales and overhead costs.
- The 'bottom line' is the final profit after all deductions including interest, tax and dividends. However, management normally make judgements on the company's performance by considering the profit before interest, tax and dividends (PBIT) and may refer to this as the 'bottom line'.
- The notes to the statutory accounts give some further information although this is quite limited.

Another financial report

So the P&L Account can tell you what the company's sales, costs and profit are. It's the balance sheet which indicates the underlying financial strength of the company.

Chapter 4 Review Questions

1   Where can you get a copy of any limited companies' statutory accounts from? When must they be filed by?

2   What is the 'bottom line' – the real one and the management version?

3   How can the material element of the cost of sales be calculated using opening and closing stock balances?

4   Define gross profit.

5   What would be the annual depreciation charge for an asset costing £2m depreciated over 10 years using the straight line method?

05

the balance sheet

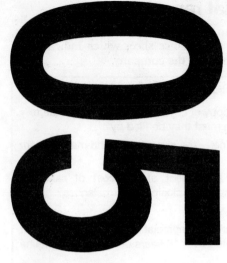

Another major report is the Balance Sheet. The Profit and Loss Account tells the informed reader how the company has performed during the period, the levels of sales, margin and costs, resulting in a certain amount of profitability. The Balance Sheet, on the other hand, indicates at how much the business is valued. Very importantly, this value is taken at the end of the accounting period.

Do realize that the Balance Sheet is only a *snapshot* of the business at a specific date. This is an important observation. It means that the day after, the figures on the balance sheet can (indeed will) change. It isn't likely to be a material difference, at least not for the first few days or weeks.

However, since management are aware that the Balance Sheet at the year end will be the one publicly available, they are usually sensible enough to make it look as good as possible, perhaps by some short-term manipulations of key figures such as cash by delaying payment to suppliers.

Given that limited companies have nine months after their financial year end to file their results at Companies House, the Balance Sheet data can be quite out of date by the time it is publicly available. Don't assume that the values in the Balance Sheet apply to the company months later, or even that the figures are in similar ratios to each other, particularly with companies operating in industries with seasonal variations in trading levels.

There are three major areas in a Balance Sheet – assets, liabilities and equity.

- *Assets* – are items either owned by the company, owed to them or something in which they have a beneficial interest.
- *Liabilities* – are items that the company owes to others, usually debts of one form or another.
- *Equity* – is deemed to be the amounts due to the owners of the company, the shareholders. It includes the profits of the company.

As a matter of course, the Balance Sheet will always balance (naturally) and all the assets will equal the sum of the liabilities and the equity. It cannot be any other way.

> A = L + E is an easy way to remember it.

The following terms make up the sections to be found on most balance sheets.

Fixed assets

Fixed assets are items acquired by the company which are not quickly consumed during the course of their use. Definitions vary from one organization to another, but most companies have authorization procedures for the acquisition of fixed assets, usually under the name of capital expenditure. A common definition is any tangible items costing £1,000 or more which will last for more than a year, although the amount does vary in different companies.

The alternative to treating a cost as a fixed asset is to expense it – deduct it from the profits in the accounting period it was acquired.

There are grey areas in the definition of fixed assets because, when the principle was established, the idea was that you had just bought a hulking great machine, something for all to see. So it would be all right to capitalize (meaning treat as a fixed asset) an expensive computer; but what about the equally expensive software? Is it tangible? You can't touch the programs, but the computer is no good without them. Some companies do capitalize software and some don't.

So would you consider any of the following to be fixed assets:
- maintenance costs on repairing a dockyard crane?
- spending £2,000 on replacing the motor of a conveyor belt?
- the architect's fees for drawing up the plans of a new office block?

The answers are no, yes (with a condition) and yes.
- The first is deemed to be a running cost (i.e. deducted from profit), because it is the nature of maintenance repairs to be done periodically, several times a year.
- The motor replacement can be added to the fixed asset register (simply a list of fixed assets acquired), but the original motor must be deducted, scrapped off.
- Architect's fees defy the definition of tangibility, but the building wouldn't proceed without the plans, so they are included. The rules aren't necessarily hard and fast – there is often considerable scope for interpretation and artistic licence!

Fixed assets are typically divided into such categories as land and buildings, plant and machinery, fixtures and fittings, and vehicles. In essence, they are items of a tangible nature that are too expensive to be deducted from the profit in the year in which they were acquired. Instead the cost of them is spread over an arbitrary lifespan given to each category (say ten years for plant and machinery), through the depreciation charge to the Profit and Loss Account.

The 'life' of the asset is, in theory, supposed to be its economic life, or how long it will last. However, this judgement is left to the directors and the easiest way to do it is to group assets together in the above categories and depreciate each category at a given rate. The usual sort of lifespans and depreciation rates you will encounter are:

Land	nil (it doesn't wear out)
Buildings	20 to 60 years (5% to 1.67%)
Plant and machinery	5 to 10 years (20% to 10%)
Fixtures and fittings	5 to 10 years (20% to 10%)
Vehicles	3 to 5 years (33% to 20%)

Of course, when the asset is fully depreciated (that is when the accumulated depreciation over the years equals the original cost of the asset and it is said to be fully written off), it does not mean that the item is no longer usable. There's many a twenty-year-old machine working away quite happily, although according to the books of the company, it has no value!

This actually caused a problem to accountants, because they felt that it meant they were understating the value of their assets on the Balance Sheet. Resourceful as ever, a new accounting rule was developed which allowed the assets to be revalued, at a figure to be determined by the directors. Of course, the auditors would require some justification for a twenty-year-old machine with a nil book value suddenly appearing on the books at £50,000, but there are professional valuers who will calculate a 'proper' value (for a fee).

A few common definitions to finish off fixed assets:

Gross book value (GBV) – is the original (historic) cost of the asset, or the revaluation amount, if it has one.

Accumulated depreciation – is the sum of the depreciation charged to the Profit and Loss Account over the years. It may be shown as:

Accumulated depreciation brought forward	£220,000
Depreciation charged to profit this year	£74,000
Accumulated depreciation carried forward	£294,000

The figure for the depreciation charged this year is the same as appears in the Profit and Loss Account under, naturally, depreciation. This is also used in the Cash Flow Statement, added back to the reconciliation because depreciation is not a cash item (see Chapter 6).

Net book value (NBV) – is the difference between the gross book value and the accumulated depreciation and is the value given to the asset in the company's accounts.

Profit/loss on disposal – is the difference between the proceeds received for a sold asset and its net book value, and appears in the P&L Account.

So for a fork lift truck costing £15,000 three years ago, depreciated over five years (at 20% depreciation p.a.) and sold for £8,000, the profit made on the disposal is:

Gross book value	£15,000
Accumulated depreciation	£9,000 (3 @ £3,000 p.a.)
Net book value	£6,000
Proceeds on sale	£8,000
Profit on disposal	£2,000

Revaluation reserve – is a section in the equity part of the Balance Sheet. This is the balancing entry to the increase in the value of the fixed assets following a revaluation exercise. By law, the directors cannot take this amount into consideration when calculating how much of the equity can be given to the shareholders as a dividend. It is a form of 'non-distributable reserve'. Only trading profits are distributable.

Leased assets – are items of a capital nature that have not been purchased outright, but have been leased from a finance company. There is, in essence, a loan from the finance company (the lessor) in order to acquire the particular asset. Interest is built into the repayments, which reduce the capital borrowed much like a repayment mortgage. At the end of the lease, all payments having been made, the title (ownership) of the asset passes to the company from the lessor.

The hire purchase or contract hire of an item is different in that ownership or title always stays with the finance company and, at the end of the contract period, the asset is handed back to the finance company (or a mere peppercorn rent paid for its continued use). Given that title will never pass to the company, the asset is excluded from the Balance Sheet – and so is the liability to pay the finance company. This is why such schemes are known as 'off balance sheet financing'.

They are, however, usually declared in a note to the accounts as 'operating leases/rentals', with a summary of the amounts the company is obliged to pay in the next year, between two to five years and beyond five years.

Goodwill – is an intangible concept of an asset. It is an accounting adjustment which basically reflects the difference between the amount a company pays to acquire another company and the book value of the assets of the purchased company as shown in its accounts.

Asset value of purchased company	£4,500,000
Consideration paid	£5,200,000
Goodwill on acquisition	£700,000

Why would you pay more for a company than its own accounts suggest it is worth? There are all sorts of strategic and commercial reasons:
- brand name
- geographic base
- customer list
- complementary products
- security of key supplies
- potential synergies
- patents and licences
- R&D technology
- management skills.

In addition, remember that the acquired company's Balance Sheet may not be a true indicator of its real value (think back to the revaluation of fixed assets).

Goodwill is created by many things, but it is essentially a question of perception. A company's books (accounts) say that it is worth one value, but an acquiring company values it differently.

Goodwill can be depreciated like a normal fixed asset, although suggested practice is now to write off the goodwill (and reduce the profits in the year) when the company is bought.

Current assets

Current assets are different from fixed assets in that they actually change quite quickly. Stock is purchased from a supplier on credit, sold to a customer who becomes a debtor. The customer pays, the payment is banked and the creditor paid. This cycle can take from a few days to several months, depending upon the nature of the business (compare a bakery to a building company).

The items included in the definition of current assets are:

Cash – how much money the organization has. This will actually differ from the current bank balance due to payments which have been lodged at the bank but that have not yet cleared the account, and issued cheques not having been processed, just like a personal account. The figure shown in the Balance Sheet is always the cash book figure, not the bank balance.

Cash is one of the key figures people tend to focus upon, quite rightly. It follows, therefore, that management, in order to impress, may attempt to ensure that the cash balance at the year end is a respectable one. Remember, the Balance Sheet shows the position of the company on a *particular day* at the end of its financial year. To achieve this, managers may delay payments to suppliers in the last few weeks of the financial year to protect the cash position.

Most people know that this goes on and that, in the first few days of the new financial year, the cash goes flying out to appease the patient creditors. So, what's the point? Does it fool anyone to inflate the cash position in this way? Apparently.

It would be more useful for a company to report its average monthly cash balance as a note to the accounts. This would give a better indication of the management's cash handling abilities, but as things stand, the closing cash position is all you get.

Trade debtors – how much the organization is owed by its customers which comes from sales invoices less credit notes and money received. This includes the VAT charged on invoices, since the customers must pay this in order for the company to pass it on to HM Customs and Excise.

Prepayments – how much the organization has paid in advance for goods and services. Normally this is a relatively small amount, but think of things like insurance or rates. The bill for the following twelve months may have to be paid all at once, but the cost of it will be spread over the year. (Remember cash v. accruals in Chapter 3?)

Stocks – also known as inventory. This is the value, at the lowest of cost or net realizable value, of the items which the company sells. The reason for the alternative method of valuing stocks is that, if the company possesses some obsolete stock that no one will buy (like Betamax video recorders), they should be valued at how much they could be sold for rather than what they cost.

Current liabilities

These are the debts of the company, payable in the relatively short term, a year or less.

Trade creditors – how much is owed to suppliers of goods and services. Some of this will have already been invoiced, but even if it has not, provision must be made by way of an 'accrual' in anticipation of the invoice. This relates back to the concept of matching the timing of recording costs to when they were incurred rather than waiting for an invoice.

As with debtors, the amounts in creditors include VAT charged by suppliers on their invoices. This input VAT can be deducted from the output VAT added to sales to form the net amount due to HM Customs and Excise.

Other creditors – how much is owed to other parties, such as VAT, PAYE, NIC, employees (if paid a week or month in hand), sundry accruals, etc.

Working capital

This term is usually the sum of the current assets less the current liabilities, although some companies do not include cash in the calculation. In theory, if the number comes out as negative, i.e. the organization's current liabilities are greater than its current assets, then the organization is in a risky position. Even if it could turn all its assets into cash, there would not be enough to meet all its liabilities. However, this is only a very general rule, since much depends on the nature of the assets and liabilities, the timing of the reports and, indeed, the type of industry. Chapter 7 on ratio analysis has examples of calculations using elements of working capital.

Net assets

Sometimes called capital employed, this is simply the sum of the fixed assets and the working capital (including cash). This figure is also used in ratio calculations, principally in working out the rate of return on capital employed (ROCE).

Long-term liabilities

The distinction between these and current liabilities is that long-term liabilities are not due for at least a year. Consequently, it will include items such as loans (but a bank overdraft would be classified as a current liability, since they are usually repayable on demand) and the amounts outstanding (obligations) on assets which have been leased rather than bought.

Equity

In theory, this is what is 'owed' to the shareholders or owners of the organization. It can comprise of:

Capital – the initial and subsequent investments by the owners, the shareholders. These are proceeds from issues of shares in the company. This definition of capital is not to be confused with capital expenditure on fixed assets.

This means a company can issue shares perhaps to finance the building and equipping of a new factory, or to raise capital to buy capital assets!

The reward for investing in a company is given to shareholders in the form of a dividend payment, but only if there are sufficient profits for the directors of the company to deem such a payment advisable. Of course, if they go too long paying small dividends or none at all, the shareholders may prefer to have new directors running the company!

Reserves – there are different types, the most common of which are:

- **Retained profits**, being the sum of all the profits made historically, less any dividends paid out. In theory, this is what the shareholders are entitled to take out of the company by way of dividends and it can be split into several categories as shown below:

Retained profits brought forward	£16,852,200
Profit this year	£2,654,600
Dividends	(£1,400,000)
Retained profits carried forward	£18,106,800

The profit for the year comes directly from the Profit and Loss Account – it is the profit after interest and tax have been deducted, but obviously before dividends (otherwise these would be deducted twice).

- **Revaluation reserve**, made when the fixed assets are restated in the accounts at a higher value than they were previously shown. Since this is just a notional accounting increase in the value of the assets and is not backed up by real money (remember this is merely someone's opinion of the value of the assets and nobody has actually bought them at that price), this cannot be taken into account when the directors come to consider how much dividend to pay out.

Preference shares – are something of a hybrid between equity and debt. They are a certain type of share in the company which allows the holder to receive interest on the investment before the holder of ordinary shares is entitled to receive a dividend. But payment is not compulsory, like it is for interest on loans. With cumulative preference shares, however, if the company does skip a payment due to lack of sufficient profits or cash, the deficit can be carried forward until it is eventually made up.

Notes to the accounts pertaining to the Balance Sheet give some analysis of the summary amounts reported in the Balance Sheet itself. Long-term creditors may be analysed by how many years ahead the amounts are due to be paid.

Intercompany debtors and creditors

Companies in the same group (with the same ultimate parent holding company) may trade with each other. Instead of showing their respective accounts in trade debtors and creditors, they are isolated as intercompany debtors and creditors. These can perhaps be taken as a measure of how much support a company gets from others in its group, particularly from its parent company if that is a substantial creditor.

Intercompany debtors and creditors appear under current assets and liabilities respectively, again because they are perceived as being settled on demand (or following an instruction from head office!).

When the accounts of the member companies are consolidated, all the intercompany balances should net out to zero and disappear.

A = L + E

Note that in the Balance Sheet, total assets always equals total liabilities plus equity. This can also be presented as total assets less total liabilities equals equity, being mathematically a rearrangement of the same equation.

Key points
- The Balance Sheet shows the value of the assets, liabilities and equity of the business on a *particular* day.
- Assets are owned by the company.
- Liabilities represent what the company owes to others.
- Equity is the shareholder's interest in the company.
- For the Balance Sheet to balance, assets = liabilities plus equity.

The last part of the statutory accounts

Although this chapter has covered the definition of items in the Balance Sheet, reading and interpreting the numbers it presents is a different matter. Chapter 7 looks at ratio analysis, using the numbers from the Balance Sheet to judge the performance of the company. Before then, there is one other key document in the accounts – the Cash Flow Statement, subject of Chapter 6.

Chapter 5 Review Questions

1 At what point in time does the Balance Sheet represent a financial statement of the company?

2 Categorize the following into assets and liabilities:
  a stocks
  b debtors
  c bank overdraft
  d trade creditors
  e capital equipment, land and buildings
  f prepayments
  g accruals.

3 What is a fixed asset? How is the cost of it charged to profits?

4 When fixed assets are revalued, their value may increase in the asset section of the Balance Sheet. Where does the other side of the entry go to maintain the principle of double entry bookkeeping?

5 How can a piece of machinery valued at £200,000 be kept off the Balance Sheet, by not being included in fixed assets?

6 Why would a company pay £5m for another company that, according to its last Balance Sheet, was only worth £4m?

7 Which items make up:
  a current assets
  b current liabilities
  c working capital
  d net assets
  e equity?

8 What formula ensures that a Balance Sheet always balances?

06

the cash flow statement

In this chapter you will lear
- how to understand the ca
  flow statement
- about cash flow and stoc
- about cash flow and prof
- about working capital, fix
  assets and cash flow

We have already established that cash is a critical factor of success to any enterprise. Profits are all very well, but a business must have cash in order to survive. The two are not necessarily automatically complementary, but both are needed for the long-term good of the firm.

The cash flow cycle

Cash comes in from customers from sales made and goes out of the business to pay suppliers for goods and services. Since such transactions are not settled immediately, there is the interim stage of debtors and creditors.

Consider the flow of cash if Lidd Enterprises, a wholesaler in laser printers, acquires ten printers at £300 each from the manufacturers at the start of January, to be paid for in four weeks time. Just two weeks later, it sells all ten at £450 each to a valued customer, who will pay in a further four weeks.

Upon receipt from the supplier, the printers go into stock while at the same time, Lidd has a creditor (the supplier). When they are sold, they move out of stock as Lidd acquires a debtor (the customer). At the end of January, cash goes out to pay the creditor, then in mid February (28 days after the sale), comes in from the debtor. The cycle looks like this:

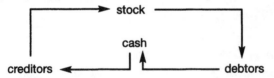

It is apparent that cash in the operating cycle either comes from debtors or goes out to creditors. Stock in itself does not create a cash movement. An increase in stock levels means higher creditors, until they are paid. A fall in stock levels gives a rise in debtors, who will eventually pay.

Non-cash items

So what causes the difference between profits and cash? In an earlier example, we looked at the timing issues involved when suppliers have to be paid before customers pay up, leading to a net outflow of cash in the short term. Over a longer period, because the amounts being received from customers are greater than those being paid out to suppliers, cash will begin to accumulate.

But when we consider the accounting profits of a company, we are dealing with a different subject. Within those neat columns of numbers, headed by £ signs, are a number of items which affect the profit, but have nothing to do with cash at all! The most significant one is usually depreciation. As explained in Chapter 4, this is an accounting convention to spread the cost of a fixed asset over more than one year. Considering the size of some items of capital expenditure (e.g. a power station), this is perfectly understandable. Even so, paying for a piece of machinery for the factory costing £100,000, which is depreciated over ten years, will only deduct £10,000 from the year's profits, but the full £100,000 from the bank account when it is paid for!

By the same token, the following year, a further £10,000 depreciation will be deducted from profit, but with nil effect on the cash position – it was all paid for in the previous year.

Similarly, the profit or loss made on the disposal of fixed assets is not a cash item. The actual proceeds received from the sale are, but the profit/loss includes the net book value of the asset at the time it was sold, after years of depreciation have been set against it. Consider a computer bought for £10,000 depreciated over five years:

Year	1	2	3	4
Cost (£)	10,000			
Depreciation (£)	2,000	2,000	2,000	2,000
Net book value (£)	8,000	6,000	4,000	2,000
Proceeds on sale (£)				3,500
Profit on disposal (£)				1,500

The depreciation is a deduction from profit each year.

Contrast the cash flows in the four years:

Year	1	2	3	4
Purchase (£)	(10,000)			
Sale (£)				3,500

A simple way of looking at cash

In its published accounts, a company will show how much it had in its cash book (the cash in the bank or the overdraft figure) at the end of its financial year and one year earlier as a comparison. It is simple to tell if it has more or less cash than it did last year.

This can be too simplistic a way of looking at the cash flow, but it generally gives a pretty good guide. It does not automatically reveal if there were loans taken out or new capital raised to bring in more cash, nor does it indicate what money was spent on. The Cash Flow Statement gives a better indication of those events.

The formal Cash Flow Statement

Under the current rules, the cash flow statement which appears as part of the company's published accounts must be analysed into five component parts:

1 Net cash flow from operating activities
2 Returns on investment and servicing of finance
3 Taxation
4 Investing activities
5 Financing

The five parts are added up to give an increase or decrease in cash and cash equivalent. The final format would look like this:

Cash Flow Statement for year ended 30 September 2006		
	£000	£000
Net cash inflow from operating activities		2,440
Returns on investments and servicing of finance		
Interest received	44	
Interest paid	(212)	
Dividends paid	(850)	
Net cash inflow from returns on investments and servicing of finance		(1,018)
Taxation		
Corporation tax paid	(331)	
Tax paid		(331)

Investing activities		
Payments for tangible fixed assets	(102)	
Receipts from sales of tangible fixed assets	27	
Net cash outflow from investing activities		(75)
Net cash inflow before financing		1,016
Financing	-	—
Increase in cash and cash equivalents		1,016

Notes to the accounts will add a little analysis to some of the figures in the Cash Flow Statement, but all the figures in the statement are taken from the Profit and Loss Account or the Balance Sheet.

The Cash Flow Statement really explains where the money has come from and gone to. It starts with the net cash inflow from operating activities, which is initially the operating profit (before taxation, interest and dividends) adjusted for any non-cash items used to reach that profit, such as depreciation. This is further adjusted by the movement in the items of working capital over the year. The changes in stock, debtors and creditors are deemed to be consumers or creators of cash, depending upon the direction in which they have moved.

An increase in stocks or debtors is deemed to reduce cash, as does a decrease in creditors (they're being paid). And vice versa for all three. A stock increase does not literally decrease cash, it would normally cause creditors to rise, but if there is not a corresponding match, then the implication is that the stock has been paid for, therefore cash has gone out of the company to the creditors.

The returns on investments and servicing of finance is a long way of saying dividends and interest, paid and received.

Taxation refers only to corporation tax, although advance corporation tax, which is triggered by the payment of dividends, is included. VAT is not, since it is included in the creditors figure.

Investing activities covers the purchase and sale of fixed assets.

Finally, financing identifies further influxes of cash from shareholders through share issues and any long-term loans taken out or repaid.

Points of interest

The way to interpret the cash flow of a company is to ask a few key questions and determine the answers from the stated figures.

Firstly, has the cash at the bank increased or otherwise? Decreases are not usually a good sign, unless the company has spent on something that appears to have profit potential, such as acquiring another company, or building another factory. However, an increase may be brought about by good cash flow management – or perhaps by taking out a loan, in order to pay for a proposed expansion. The answers have to be looked for, but they can be found.

A good place to start is the working capital. Very broadly speaking, assuming that trading conditions have not radically altered, stocks, debtors and creditors ought to be roughly in line with sales, comparing year to year. If debtors have risen relatively, it may, just may, suggest that longer credit terms have been offered to customers to secure sales. If creditors have gone up too, then they are the ones who are paying for it!

Then look at fixed asset purchases. Is money being spent on the future of the company? Is it as much as last year, bearing in mind that some investments in assets may occur only every twenty years or more, such as building a new factory for increased production capacity?

There's not much that can be done about tax and interest payments, although tax planning can minimize the former. The only way to pay less interest is to owe less.

Which leads nicely to looking at the movement in loans, whether they have increased or fallen; similarly with issues of capital to raise money from shareholders. Injections of large amounts of cash can be required by a company for two reasons – to finance an expansion of one sort or another which is so large that current cash amounts are insufficient to finance it; or to keep the creditors at bay so they don't have the company bankrupted and wound up out of existence. Interpret the Profit and Loss Account, the Balance Sheet and the Cash Flow Statement to decide which way it is.

Key points
- Profit and cash are not the same thing, nor does one necessarily imply the other.
- Depreciation is a significant charge to profits that has no cash effect. Buying a fixed asset can represent a major drain in cash, but its effect on profit is spread over several years through depreciation.
- When examining a company's accounts for the cash information, start with the simplest analysis – the cash at bank or overdraft figure, and the change in it from last year.
- Then consider the movements in the elements of working capital. Has a reduction in cash been brought about by increased stocks for which the suppliers have been paid?
- Two outside sources of cash are loan or funding from shareholders (through share issues).

Using figures

The facts and figures have been presented in the forms of the Profit and Loss Account, the Balance Sheet and the Cash Flow Statement. Next you need to be able to understand what those figures are telling you, through ratio analysis.

Chapter 6 Review Questions

1 What are the sources of cash – in the daily routine of business (the operating cycle) and elsewhere?

2 Would purchasing more stock imply an immediate reduction in cash?

3 How would the purchase of a fixed asset for £10,000, depreciated over five years, affect
   a profit
   b cash?

ratio analysis

In this chapter you will learn
- about what the statutory reports tell you
- how to establish a point of reference
- about sales ratios and what they tell you
- about operating profit, ROCE and other ratios
- about management ratios
- about how investors and lenders use ratios

Making sense of the numbers

So there you are, having been presented with a set of accounts on a competitor, or even your own company, and you want to know what it all means.

From the Profit and Loss Account, you know what the sales, margin and profit are. The Balance Sheet reveals useful information like cash/loans, debtors and creditors.

But what do these numbers really tell you?

A general theory of relativity

Suppose Columbus Explorers Limited, an established firm of map makers, declared in their latest accounts that they had sales of £8,010,402 in the last financial year and profits of £309,820. Is that a good result?

Would your answer change if you knew any of the following beforehand?
- The budget for the year was sales of £12,500,000 and a profit of £316,250.
- The year before, the company sold £7,852,236 with profits of £370,950.
- The market leader has sales of £18,000,000.

Any number in isolation does not give much of an indication as to the quality of the result – there must be a point of reference to enable us to make a judgement.

All financial figures need to be interpreted in comparison with other figures, whether they be historical for the company or set against competitors' or industry averages. On its own, a sales performance of £8,010,402 could be good, bad or indifferent. Measured against a benchmark, it is given meaning.

A different way of looking at the same numbers

Ratio analysis is simply a way of looking at the numbers of a company in relation to each other, but the same point must be made as above. Ratios need to be viewed in a context to have meaning.

Return on sales

A key ratio is the *return on sales* percentage, which is the profit divided by the sales expressed as a percentage. Columbus may have a return on sales of 4%, but you don't know whether to praise or condemn the management for their efforts unless that figure is compared with something else. If the industry average is 3%, hurrah! Last year they achieved 4.7%, bad news!

But the budget was to make 2.5% – good. All is relative. Bearing that in mind, let us turn to how to combine the numbers from the Profit and Loss Account and the Balance Sheet to provide some meaningful ratios.

The beauty of using ratios is precisely that it does allow comparative measurements of different sized firms. A firm with half of the sales of another may make a better percentage profit, which will be clearly evident by comparing the appropriate ratios.

Everything divided by sales

The easy ratios to start with are all the lines in the P&L Account as a percentage of the sales figure. These often appear in management reports and give a guide to the relative importance of different areas of the business. For instance, consider the following P&L Account:

Columbus Explorers Limited
Profit and Loss Account for the year ended 31 March 2006

	£	%
Sales	8,010,402	
Cost of sales	4,204,696	52.5
Margin	3,805,706	47.5
Overheads:		
Production	679,232	8.5
Distribution	406,212	5.0
Sales force	701,844	8.8
Marketing	496,450	6.2
R&D	320,404	4.0
Finance	198,680	2.5
Administration	282,301	3.5
Depreciation	281,005	3.5
Total overheads	3,366,128	42.0
Profit before interest and taxation	439,578	5.5
Interest payable	47,269	0.6
Taxation	82,489	1.0
Profit after interest and taxation	309,820	3.9

Isn't it easier to absorb the information in the % column rather than the bare numbers?

However, do be aware that, on their own, the percentages are insufficient to make any grand assumptions about performance. The sales force cost 8.8% of the sales revenue – if Columbus cut back the costs in that area, would sales fall? How much would sales increase by if we added £50,000 to the marketing costs? Such questions are not answered here, but the percentages can give an indication of areas of concern, especially if the trend is considered year on year.

Similarly, if the market leader in the industry spends 12% of its sales figure on its sales force, should Columbus follow suit? It's all comparative and relative.

Review the above comments bearing in mind last year's financial information (supplied below). Work out the percentages for yourself.

Columbus Explorers Limited
Profit and Loss Account for the year ended 31 March 2006

	31.3.06 £	31.3.05 £
Sales	8,010,402	7,852,236
Cost of sales	4,204,696	4,177,387
Margin	3,805,706	3,674,849
Overheads:		
Production	679,232	654,956
Distribution	406,212	410,852
Sales force	701,844	654,655
Marketing	496,450	465,267
R&D	320,404	194,705
Finance	198,680	194,352
Administration	282,301	289,514
Depreciation	281,005	275,652
Total overheads	3,366,128	3,139,953
Profit before interest and taxation	439,578	534,896
Interest payable	47,269	65,281
Taxation	82,489	98,665
Profit after interest and taxation	309,820	370,950

Sales divided by everything

Columbus Explorers Limited
Balance Sheet as at 31 March 2006

	31.03.06 £	31.03.05 £
Fixed assets		
Gross book value	6,245,742	6,178,965
Accumulated depreciation	2,425,696	2,144,691
Net book value	3,820,046	4,034,274
Current assets		
Stocks	612,550	589,365
Debtors	3,254,522	2,740,005
Cash at bank	440,548	112,450
Current liabilities		
Creditors	2,875,612	2,520,948
Net current assets	1,432,008	920,872
Total net assets	5,252,054	4,955,146
Shareholders funds		
Capital	10,000	10,000
Profit reserves	2,854,612	2,544,792
Revaluation reserve	812,000	812,000
Total shareholders funds	3,676,612	3,366,792
Long-term liabilities		
Loan	1,500,000	1,500,000
Creditors due after more than one year	75,442	88,354
Total long-term liabilities	1,575,442	1,588,354
Total capital employed	5,252,054	4,955,146

This is a summary Balance Sheet for Columbus. Detailed analysis of some of the figures would be available, some as notes to the accounts, some only in management reports. Debtors would be broken down into trade debtors and prepayments, creditors into trade creditors, accruals, VAT, etc.

The converse of using the Profit and Loss Account lines divided by sales is to take the figures from the Balance Sheet and divide them into the sales figure.

Sales over total net assets gives a number which provides an indication of how well the assets of the company are being used. (For Columbus, the number is 1.28.)

After all, stocks and debtors should be dependent upon sales, creditors should fluctuate with the cost of sales and hence sales, and fixed assets tend to be production based, which ought to help increase sales in the end. The common phrase is how much are the assets 'made to sweat' and this ratio implies how well the assets are being managed – the lower the number, the better, i.e. high sales are achieved without needing too much capital. Remember though, it should be a comparative measure – to last year, a competitor, the budget, whatever. A ratio of 1.28 doesn't tell you anything much by itself.

You can then go on to divide all the Balance Sheet items into the sales figure. The total operating assets are the net current assets and the fixed assets. Work those ratios out.

Net current assets are made up of stocks, debtors, creditors and cash – calculate the sales ratio for each of them. See if a trend is developing for any given ratio. Is one element playing a more important role than another? The ratios may not give you the right answer immediately, but they can lead you to ask the right question.

	Ratios	
	31.3.06	31.3.05
Fixed assets		
Gross book value	1.28	1.27
Accumulated depreciation	3.30	3.67
Net book value	1.66	1.95
Current assets		
Stocks	13.08	13.32
Debtors	2.46	2.86
Cash at bank	18.18	69.83
Current liabilities:		
Creditors	2.79	3.11
Net current assets	5.59	8.52
Total net assets	1.52	1.58
Shareholders interests		
Capital	801.01	785.23
Profit reserves	2.08	3.08
Revaluation reserve	9.86	9.67
Total shareholders interests	1.71	2.33
Long-term liabilities		
Loan	5.34	5.23
Creditors due after more than one year	106.18	88.87
Total long-term liabilities	5.08	4.94
Total capital employed	1.52	1.58

These ratios are of limited use on their own, but give an indication of the relative importance of various parts of the Balance Sheet in their relationship to sales. In some cases, there may not be a direct connection to sales – fixed assets for instance. That said, it is the change in the ratio that attracts attention.

ROCE

Often the very first ratio calculated by a keen analyst of published accounts is the return on capital employed (ROCE).

Its formula is very simple:

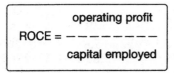

$$ROCE = \frac{operating\ profit}{capital\ employed}$$

Operating profit is the same as the profit before interest and tax.

The ROCE for Columbus is 439,578/5,252,054 = 8.36% (2005 was 10.79%).

Unfortunately, the definition of capital employed is not always the same and the analyst can use total capital, or exclude current liabilities (long-term capital), shareholders' equity capital (ordinary share capital plus reserves) or one of several other options. However, the first definition, total assets, is normally used, but do watch out for variations.

Of course, a different number in the bottom part of the equation will give a different answer, but that is not necessarily too important as long as the same definition is used consistently. That will at least give a reasonable basis for comparison.

Similarly, the operating profit is usually taken as being before tax and interest, but could, if required, include either or both.

All of which is to say that a ROCE of 8% might be good or bad depending upon what it was last year, what the budget was, how competitors fared, etc.

Do bear in mind that the accounts are prepared on a historic cost basis, which will distort the true value of the fixed assets in particular. If revalued figures are available, they may give a more meaningful ratio.

Other ratios – quickly

Probably, the next thing our inquisitive analyst would consider is the current ratio, then the quick ratio.

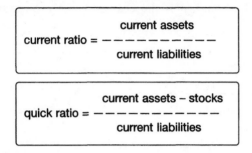

$$\text{current ratio} = \frac{\text{current assets}}{\text{current liabilities}}$$

$$\text{quick ratio} = \frac{\text{current assets} - \text{stocks}}{\text{current liabilities}}$$

For Columbus, these work out to be:

current ratio = 4,307,620/2,875,612 = 1.50 (2005 was 1.37)
quick ratio = 3,695,070/2,875,612 = 1.28 (2005 was 1.13).

The first ratio considers the relative size of the elements of the working capital. There is no right figure, because it depends upon the industry, the time of the year, the state of the business etc. However, it goes some way to answering an important question: if the company were to be wound up and all its assets turned into cash, would all the money due from its customers (debtors) plus sale of all the stock (at cost) plus whatever cash is in the bank be enough to pay off the creditors? If the current ratio is 1 or more, then yes. Below 1, then no. To have a degree of comfort in the short-term financial strength of the company, a ratio of between 1.2 to 1.8 is often considered reasonable. So Columbus can be said to look reasonably healthy.

The quick ratio (also known as the acid test) is a little more draconian, because it doesn't allow for stock. Debtors are normally turned into cash fairly quickly and it is reasonable to assume that most of them will be turned to cash eventually.

Meanwhile, stock may take six months to go through production to become sales and then debtors. Also, if the company really did have to sell its stock, enterprising purchasers would undoubtedly take advantage to secure it at less than its original cost.

So is the sum of debtors and cash together enough to settle current liabilities? The norm, subject to all the other things mentioned previously, is 0.8 to 1.2 for the quick ratio. Again, Columbus looks as though it has got things under control.

Useful management ratios

A good one that accountants like to show to sales directors is the debtor days ratio. This shows how many days' sales are represented by the debtors figure. The lower the better, because it implies that the customers aren't getting very long credit terms, so the cash is coming in quicker.

$$\text{debtor days} = \frac{\text{debtors}}{\text{sales in the year (with VAT)}} \times 365$$

Why add VAT to the sales figure? Because it is already included in the debtors figure. A sale of £1,000 becomes an invoice to the customer for £1,175 at the UK standard rate of VAT.

Of course, not all sales will have VAT added – export sales don't attract VAT, neither do sales of certain exempt or zero-rated products. So there might be some guesswork involved, or you could just leave the VAT out of it after all. If you are comparing the ratios for this year and last, then in all likelihood, the pattern of sales subject to VAT would be similar, just make sure you are treating the two years consistently. Only if the company had suddenly gone into exports in a big way (or come out of exports) would the exclusion of VAT become a significant factor.

The debtor days for Columbus is (assuming all sales are standard VAT rated):

$$\frac{3,254,522}{8,010,402 \times 1.175} \times 365 = 126 \text{ days}$$
(2005 was 108 days).

This means that the equivalent of 126 days' worth of sales remained unpaid for at the year end. If Columbus had standard credit terms of 120 days to customers, all would seem well. If it only offers 30 days as a rule, then its credit collection procedures would seem ineffective.

However, this result could hide any fluctuations in sales or debt collection in the period, so a more accurate indication of the latest position is to take the sales in a shorter recent accounting period, say the last month, multiplying the ratio by 28 days (or as appropriate) to get the debtor days:

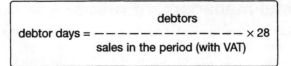

$$\text{debtor days} = \frac{\text{debtors}}{\text{sales in the period (with VAT)}} \times 28$$

Unfortunately, we are not in a position to be able to calculate this (we don't have detailed sales figures), although management would be. Columbus may have relatively high debtors to sales because it is a seasonal business and gets most of its sales in the last couple of months of the year. The 28-day based calculation would give a better indication if the information was available.

Similarly, creditor days will indicate how long before a supplier gets paid, on average (using cost of sales and overhead costs, excluding labour and depreciation). Payment of individual suppliers will vary from this figure, but it is interesting to compare creditor days with the debtors days to see how long the company generally hangs on to the money collected before parting with it.

The person responsible for cash flow management (usually the head of Finance) likes to see debtors days much lower than creditor days. A company with standard sales terms of 30 days will probably have debtor days between 35 and 45 with good credit control. The extra days are caused by customers with extended credit terms and reluctant payers.

Creditor days is firmly in the company's control – it pays out when it wants (subject to pressure from its creditors).

In a similar vein, there is a calculation for stock to indicate how often it is replenished on average. The stock turnover ratio is

$$\text{stock turnover} = \frac{\text{cost of goods sold}}{\text{stock}}$$

Columbus reports a stock ratio of 4,204,696 / 612,550 = 6.86 (2005 was 7.09).

The calculation can be done for groups of product, not just the whole stock, if the figures are available.

With the stock turnover ratio, the higher the better – that is, stock once received isn't sitting around in the warehouse waiting to be processed or sold. It's rushed into production and out to customers and so turned into cash that much earlier (via debtors).

These three are all pretty good measures of management's control of their working capital.

Ratios for lenders and investors

Gearing is one previously referred to and is much beloved by professional analysts and those who like to use buzz words to impress. It is a figure which tells us who is putting the money into the company, the shareholders who own it or lenders, usually banks. The standard formula is

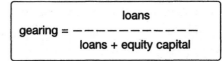

$$\text{gearing} = \frac{\text{loans}}{\text{loans} + \text{equity capital}}$$

Columbus has a gearing of 1,500,000 / (1,500,000 + 3,676,612) = 28.9% (2005 was 30.8%).

A very high figure (over 80%) may make investors and lenders nervous about advancing further sums, because loans tend to be expensive and a drain on profits. A low figure may imply cautious management, a cash rich company or simply that management hasn't yet identified a worthwhile project requiring large medium- or long-term borrowings.

The lenders are also very keen on knowing what the interest cover is, or put another way, how many times the profits of the company could have paid the interest charge:

$$\text{interest cover} = \frac{\text{profit before interest and tax}}{\text{interest charged}}$$

The interest cover for Columbus is 439,578 / 47,269 = 9.3 (2005 was 8.2).

The higher this is, the more often the company would have been capable of paying its interest charges. It gives a higher level of comfort to potential investors if the rate is 9.3 rather than 1.4.

Similarly shareholders and potential investors will work out the dividend cover:

$$\text{dividend cover} = \frac{\text{profit after tax} - \text{preference dividends}}{\text{equity dividend declared}}$$

This does not apply to Columbus, which has no preference shares, nor did it pay a dividend this year.

Profit after tax (PAT) is used because the shareholders are the last ones to have a claim on the profits. The higher this ratio is, the more likely the company is able to maintain dividend payments and therefore be a more attractive investment opportunity.

There are other ratios quoted in the financial press which are generally of limited concern of the management in their day-to-day running of the company. However, the shareholders are interested in dividend yields, earnings per share (EPS) and price earnings (P/E) ratios, and they want to see good ones. Since in theory they employ the directors, then the directors ought to have a concern for these numbers, especially if they are shareholders themselves.

$$\text{dividend yield} = \frac{\text{dividend}}{\text{share price}}$$

$$\text{earnings per share (EPS)} = \frac{\text{profit after tax} - \text{preference dividend}}{\text{number of ordinary shares issued}}$$

$$\text{price earnings (P/E) ratio} = \frac{\text{market price per share}}{\text{earnings per share}}$$

Note that the dividend yield and P/E ratio are capable of being quite volatile, as the market price for any share quoted on the stock exchange can change quickly.

The dividend yield gives an indication of the potential return on an investment in the shares (in the same way that a building society account can declare a return of 5% interest).

The P/E is normally used to compare the company with others in the same industry, using the logic that companies with high earnings per share are capable of paying out handsome dividends. They make attractive investment opportunities, so the shares are highly valued and accordingly highly priced. In theory.

Unfortunately since management are aware of this aspect of share trading, and may be judged by these ratios (among other criteria), there have been suggestions that this prompts them into short-term thinking. They may be tempted to pursue policies that make quick profits to support the share price, but which may be to the detriment of the long-term profitability of the company.

Apples and apples

Companies can be different shapes and sizes, but you can still use ratio analysis to compare them with each other. The only caution is that companies don't always define any given term, such as profit, in the same way as other companies.

We've already seen that the profit depends upon the accounting policies used, such as depreciation and capitalisation of interest. Take R&D costs too – do these always, or only sometimes, include all R&D staff costs, maintenance of R&D technical equipment, an allocation of central computer and administration costs, etc?

'A strong and healthy Balance Sheet'

This is a common phrase, but it means different things to different people. Generally a balance sheet can be considered to be 'strong' and 'healthy' to the extent that it shows:
• a positive working capital
• positive net assets
• 'substantial' profit reserves
• relatively low loans/borrowings (low gearing).

All this is, of course, subject to the nature of the business, the industry in which it operates, any seasonal fluctuations, amongst other circumstances. That said, there are Balance Sheets which can look distinctly weak and unwell!

Key points

- A point of reference must be established in order to make worthwhile comparisons. It can be last year's figures, a budget, another company, the industry average or upper quartile, but there must be a benchmark.
- Using the Profit and Loss Account, dividing the various lines by sales can help managers to focus on areas of strength or concern.
- Using the Balance Sheet, dividing the various lines into sales gives an indication of the relative importance of the items in the Balance Sheet, although only loose interpretations can be applied.
- The principle ratios are the return on capital employed (ROCE) and the current ratio.
- Lenders will be concerned about gearing and interest cover.
- Investors will look at dividend cover and yield, and the EPS and P/E ratios.

Who wants to know?

Many different numbers are available in the Profit and Loss Account, the Balance Sheet and the Cash Flow Statement. They can be understood by ratio analysis, in comparison to prior years, other companies, budgets and plans.

But who's interested? Who wants to know? There are different sets of people with varying reasons for wanting to know.

Chapter 7 Review Questions

1 Why wouldn't knowing that Columbus had sales of £8m be very useful in measuring the company's performance?

2 What is the most common definition of the return on capital employed?

3 Differentiate between the current and quick ratios.

4 If a company's standard credit terms are 30 days, what might cause the debtor days ratio to be 44 days?

5 Is it better for the stock turnover ratio to increase or decrease?

6 What ratios will interest potential lenders to the company?

7 What ratios will investors calculate?

08

users of
financial
information

In this chapter you will learn
- who the stakeholders are
- about accounts and their users
- how managers present their financial information

Finding the accounts

All limited companies must, by law, send copies of their statutory accounts to Companies House in Cardiff (or Edinburgh as appropriate, see Appendix C), within nine months of their financial year end. There are penalties for those who do not do so, with fines levied upon the directors.

Once the information has been lodged there, it is literally in the public domain, for such information is available to anyone for a small fee.

But who would be interested? Why? And what would they be interested in particularly?

The stakeholders

Any party that has a concern in the results of a company is deemed to be a 'stakeholder'. Some of them are obvious – shareholders for instance. Others want to know what's been going on too, for their own vested interests.

Competitors

Companies like to know what the opposition has been up to. They will use the results as a point of comparison for their own achievements, concentrating on sales, margin and profitability. Wouldn't you do the same with a copy of their accounts?

Also, in the notes to the accounts, there are often specific details like R&D and advertising expenditure. This might be nice to know as a guide to setting a company's own future budgets in these areas, but it must allow for the fact that it does not know the precise basis or contents of the figures quoted! Just copying the competition isn't the recommended way of setting a budget, but if you knew that a competitor with more sales than you put £250,000 into advertising last year against your £110,000, would it influence you?

Customers

A business ought to make a profit. The alternative is to make a loss which could lead to the company's demise. But customers don't like their suppliers to make too much of a profit, because it is deemed to be at their expense. If profits are unacceptably high, for whatever reason, the customers may feel that the supplier should be able to offer lower prices.

In contrast, customers will also be concerned about the long-term viability of their suppliers. Excessive profit is one thing but, without *some* profit, the supplier isn't going to be around for long enough to be able to build and sustain a good long-term working partnership with the customer. Therefore, customers will be happiest with a 'reasonable' level of profit – a term which is highly subjective and probably with a fluctuating definition.

In the same vein, many customers are wary of the supplier being too reliant upon them – if one customer represents anything above 10% of the total sales, loss of the account would prove damaging to the supplier, if not catastrophic. Rather than allow that to happen, many firms would rather diversify their sources than put a supplier at risk.

Hence, customers who analyse the accounts will tend to focus on sales and profit.

Employees

Staff are interested in knowing three things about their company – its continued viability, its progress from last year and its profitability. The first will indicate that their jobs are relatively safe; the second whether they are even safer or whether the trend points to the reverse; the third aspect causes the employees to react like customers – if excessive profits are being made, it could be at their expense and next time they will want a fairer share of it (and why not?).

Profit is the key element here, although employees may be interested, by way of comparison with their own earnings, in the note to the accounts that reveals the remuneration of the directors. This is not done by named individual, but can throw up some interesting discrepancies between the earnings of directors and employees!

Bankers, suppliers and credit agencies

These are all concerned with how safe their money will be if they lend to the company, supply goods on credit or, in the case of credit agencies, how safe they think other people's money will be. The checks are made on the company's viability and creditworthiness, by considering interest cover, creditor days, current ratio, quick ratio and gearing, in addition to the profit line and the cash flow.

When considering whether to give a customer credit terms (or how much to set for a credit limit), these are the areas of the accounts to concentrate on.

Investment brokers, City analysts, financial press

If the company is quoted on the Stock Exchange, this group will be interested in investment ratios such as earnings per share, P/E ratio, dividend yield and cover, trends in profits, gearing and cash flow.

Potential employees and shareholders will look for the same things as existing ones.

Anyone else?

There are organizations which calculate industry-based statistics, using the results of companies within particular sectors. They then compile and sell that information, often with the comparative figures for the specific company making the data purchase. The usual application is for credit insurance purposes, but it can also be applied to investment potential, in comparing the performance of a company with its sector.

Not everyone is concerned purely with the financial results of a company. The published accounts of a plc are a public relations opportunity, and can be presented in a glossy brochure with lots of information about the company and a statement from the chairman. This statement will inevitably refer to the need to contain costs (especially payroll costs) in order to remain competitive in a difficult market – even if the company had an enormously successful year!

The people in the local community might be interested in the contents of the brochure, as well as the financial results. Hints at expansion may be welcomed (bringing increased employment) or disapproved of (for example, if there are environmental concerns), or there may be the possibility of closure of certain sites.

Many users, one set of accounts

Given that all these different people are examining the accounts, looking for different things, how should the company go about revealing what has actually happened?

Usually by including as little as possible!

Companies tend to disclose the minimum they are obliged to do so by law. Why should they tell competitors how much they have spent on product development, or what lines are profitable? Rather than give such an advantage to their competitors, they give away nothing if they can.

Financial results can be clouded by interpretation, reclassification and judgement, ignoring any debatable accounting tricks (see Chapter 15). Be aware that you might not always be comparing apples with apples – as we have already established, calculations to derive profit vary!

Other sources of information – financial or otherwise

- **Trade exhibitions** – what does the company's display tell you? How does it compare to its competitors?
- **Trade associations** – ask them what they can tell you about the company.
- **Visit the company** – you can learn a great deal from looking round a company's operations and talking to its employees.
- **Customers and suppliers** – each will have their own opinion about the company.
- **The media** – trade magazines and journals (e.g. *The Grocer* for retailers), the financial press and local newspapers do occasionally report things which may be relevant to your enquiries. Check out the company newsletter for a more favourable presentation.

Read the small print

It is common to find in advertisements for financial investment opportunities the phrase, 'Past performance is not a guarantee of future returns'. This is true of company accounts too – at best they can only be taken as a guide.

Key points

- Different groups of people make up the 'stakeholders' –
  everyone and anyone with an interest in a company. Each
  group has its own interests and its own reasons for
  analysing the company's figures, and they may concentrate
  on different parts of the accounts as a result.
- Given this diversity of readers, most companies try to
  choose the safest and easiest route by declaring as little
  information as they can legally get away with.
- However, the financial information obtained from the
  accounts can be supplemented by non-financial news from
  other sources.

The fount of all knowledge

We've seen the reports with the numbers, we've looked at how
to interpret them and considered who's interested in finding out
what. But where do the numbers come from? Under the direct
control of the Accounts department, the source of the
information is the general ledger.

Chapter 8 Review Questions

1 How long can companies wait before they must submit
  accounts to Companies House to avoid legal penalties?

2 Why would the following groups be interested in the financial
  results of a company:
  a competitors
  b customers
  c suppliers
  d employees
  e lenders
  f investors and their advisers?

3 Where could you get non-financial information from?

09 the general ledger

The centre of the universe

As far as accountants are concerned, the general ledger is the fount of all financial information. They are (mostly) not foolish enough to believe that it contains all the answers to all of the questions, but a well structured general ledger can provide much useful financial information to management to help in running the company. In essence, the contents of the general ledger form the accounts.

A system of financial recording

The general ledger is the bucket into which the financial effects of all transactions are poured. They can then be extracted in intelligible reports to be used for decision making.

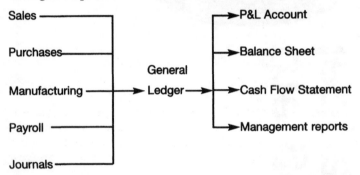

In any business there is usually a lot going on – sales and purchasing activities could number hundreds or thousands a week. The transactions from any system can be entered (posted is the accounting term) to the general ledger either individually or in batches, depending upon the nature of the computer software or, for a manual system, the desires of the accountant. Mostly they are done in batches, purely because of the sheer volume of transactions which take place.

For instance, a company might be termed small if it has sales of £5m a year, but if its average order is £500, there will be about 10,000 sales invoices a year; around 900 a month. Rather than fill up the ledger with 900 postings, they might be summarized into daily or even weekly batches and posted as batch totals.

The detail should also be recorded in reports where the individual postings are listed.

Sources of financial data

The three principal activities of a manufacturing organization are buying, making and selling. Other companies skip the middle one.

It is, therefore, no surprise that buying and selling have their own financial recording systems, the purchase and sales ledgers respectively. These establish the causes of money flowing out of and into the company (payments from/to debtors and creditors). Manufacturing doesn't usually have a separate system for financial purposes, since the major concern is with quantities and turning volumes of raw materials into units of finished goods.

These two primary financial systems link in to the general ledger, or in computer parlance, they interface. From the sales ledger, sales invoices will be posted as:
- debit debtors (that's easy to remember)
- credit sales.

We are back to the double entry idea again!

Transactions from the purchase ledger will always credit creditors (unless it's a credit note, which debits the purchase ledger) and the debit will depend upon the type of expenditure. Purchases of stock will go to a stock account (in the Balance Sheet), items of an overhead (expense) nature will be charged (debited) to the appropriate section of the Profit and Loss Account.

Control accounts

In fact, both the debtors and creditors accounts in the general ledger are key control accounts. They are so called because the balance of each of them is a check on the proper functioning of the interfaces, since they must each be the same as the total of their respective sales/purchase ledgers. Any invoice raised on a customer's account in the sales ledger must be reflected as a transaction in the control account in the general ledger.

Similarly, when payment is received from customers, the amount is set against the appropriate invoices in the sales ledger and in the general ledger:
- debit cash
- credit debtors control account.

This is a good point to introduce another control account – the cash account in the general ledger. Its balance should be the same as that of the cash book, whether it is kept on a computer or in a real book. The transactions are either payments or receipts and, so long as they are posted to the general ledger (payments as credits, receipts as debits), then the two should remain perfectly synchronized.

This may seem the wrong way round, payment being a credit. When you pay money into your personal bank account, it shows as a credit on the statement. But from the bank's view, it has a corresponding debit entry – it owes you money; it is your debtor (or you are its creditor).

Relationships with other systems

There are other operations in the company which have a financial impact that are posted to the general ledger. This can be done either automatically on a computer if there is a program which sends the data to the general ledger, either in batches or in detail. Or, if the program for the operation is not integrated with the general ledger, the results can be posted using a journal. Of course, if the general ledger is a manual (book) one, figures have to be written in anyway.

Payroll

The financial elements of the payroll go beyond the gross pay figure. The company pays national insurance and pension contributions, which are further costs. Also, employees pay tax and sometimes their own pension contributions, not forgetting there may be other deductions before arriving at net pay, including union dues, hospital fund, Give As You Earn, etc.

Even the gross pay may be analysed into basic pay plus overtime (at various premium rates), bonuses, first aid allowances and so on.

All these amounts must be posted to the general ledger. This can be done by individual employee, summarized by department or just lumped all together into one big payroll cost. It depends what information is sought from the general ledger. There's no point in carefully constructing the general ledger and payroll interface to show overtime costs at five different premium rates if all anyone ever asks is 'What's the total overtime this month?'

The debit entries are for the gross pay costs and the employer's national insurance and pension contributions. The credits go into the Balance Sheet part of the general ledger, usually somewhere among the sundry creditors section, because these represent amounts that are owed to someone else – net pay to employees, pension contributions to the pension fund, tax and NIC to the Inland Revenue/DSS.

Production system

Although not principally a financial system, the production system does produce relevant data for the accounts. These are to do with:

- receiving raw materials (debit raw materials, credit goods received not invoiced);
- issuing of raw materials into the production process (debit work-in-progress, credit raw materials);
- receiving finished goods from production (debit finished goods, credit work-in-progress).

Physical stock flow and accounting for it

Debit:	Raw materials	Work in progress	Finished goods	Debtors
Supplier:	Raw materials	Work in progress	Finished goods	Customer
Credit:	Creditors	Raw materials	Work in progress	Finished goods

The values will not stay the same as the product flows along. The company adds value to the raw materials by processing them into finished goods.

Journal entries

The other way entries are made to the general ledger (or entries already in there altered) lies directly in the control of the Accounts – the journal.

This is simply a form upon which the accounts to be debited and credited are written, together with the amounts involved. As ever, the total debits must equal the total credits. Any half-decent general ledger software will not allow a journal that doesn't balance to be entered.

A journal may look like this:

Journal – StopOne Limited

Accounting Period: December 2006
Journal Number: 412
Date of entry: 2/1/07
Description: Year end adjustments

Account Code	Dr (£)	Cr (£)	Description
500/2300	5,000.00		Packaging
400/2300		5,000.00	Coding error
100/4000	1,250.00		Discount for engine
000/3620		1,250.00	Discount for engine
Total	6,250.00	6,250.00	

The parts in bold are standard to every journal form this company uses. The accountant, or one of her staff, fill in the rest as appropriate.

Note that the date of entry is not the same as the accounting period. In fact it is usually a little later, because journals tend to be done after the period end, so the accounts people can get a look at what has gone into the general ledger from other systems, before using journals to try and sort them out. Transactions may have gone to the wrong account, or perhaps somebody didn't book in a delivery of goods and the transaction needs to be reflected in the right period in the general ledger.

There are two main kinds of journal – ordinary and reversing. An ordinary one puts its debits and credits into a single accounting period and that's it.

A reversing journal puts the postings into a period, then reverses them back out (swaps round the debits and credits) in a later period, usually the next one. But what is the point of putting them in and taking them out again?

It's to do with the matching principle – recording the financial effect of the transactions in the period in which they occur, not when the invoice catches up. If you know the invoice is coming the following month, a reversing journal is just the trick. In the first period, the journal is really creating an accrual:

    April   – debit consultancy fees £1,000
              – credit sundry creditors/accruals £1,000.

The following month, the invoice arrives and is posted:

May   – debit consultancy fees £1,000
       – credit creditors £1,000.

Leaving it like this would mean two sets of consultancy fees are charged to the accounts!

But the reversing journal comes into play:

May   – debit sundry creditors/accruals £1,000
       – credit consultancy fees £1,000.

The net result is that one lot of fees are charged to expenses in April and a real creditor is recognized in May, as can be seen by an enquiry in to the general ledger accounts:

Consultancy fees:			
			£
April	Journal	**Dr**	1,000
May	Invoice	**Dr**	1,000
	R/Journal	**Cr**	1,000
	Net	**Dr**	1,000
Sundry creditors:			
			£
April	Journal	**Cr**	1,000
May	R/Journal	**Dr**	1,000
	Net		–
Trade creditors:			
			£
May	Invoice	**Cr**	1,000

Chart of accounts

Rather than use descriptions like debtors control and consultancy fees to label the individual accounts in the general ledger, it is much easier to refer to them by an account code. This is usually a number, although it can include letters.

As we have seen, related types of expenditure can be grouped together:

        3000 – Electricity
        3010 – Gas
        3020 – Fuel oil
        3030 – Water
        3040 – Acid

These are examples of expense codes. They can be structured so that all maintenance expense codes start with a 2, all labour-related ones with a 4, making summary reporting so much easier. The length of the code is determined by the software used for the general ledger.

To know which department is incurring that cost, there is also a department code:

> 200 – Warehouse
> 250 – Machine shop
> 300 – Assembly
> 350 – Plating
> 400 – Inspection

So, if the Plating department buys some acid, the appropriate code for the cost, to which the invoice must be 'coded up', is 350/3040.

In some general ledger structures it might be the other way round, with the expense part of the code first. Additional parts of the code may be required, for example for the particular company (if more than one company are sharing the general ledger software) or for a division of the company.

The chart of accounts is simply a list of all the account codes that can be used:

Code	Description
100/2000	Production – Basic pay
100/2010	Production – Overtime
100/2020	Production – NIC
.	
.	
.	
100/4500	Production – depreciation (P&M)
200/2000	Distribution – basic pay
200/2010	Distribution – overtime
and so on.	

The expense code always stands for the same type of cost, just as the department code for, say, Distribution is always consistent.

The list of available account codes is maintained by the Accounts department, which can create new ones as required. People who use the codes include the Accounts staff and anyone responsible for purchasing goods and services, as they can determine where the cost should be directed in the general ledger. This is usually done at the time of raising a purchase order, or subsequently. The invoice itself can be posted to the appropriate general ledger account (via the purchase ledger system).

The trial balance

The aim is to report the financial information captured in the general ledger and the basic document for this is the trial balance.

Simply, this is a listing of all the account codes (from the chart of accounts) with the values they currently hold. Some reports may also show the movement or change in the account during the period.

The following abbreviations are used:

FA	= Fixed assets
L&B	= Land and buildings
P&M	= Plant and machinery
RM	= Raw materials
FG	= Finished goods
QC	= Quality control

Trial balance for ABC Limited at 31 May 2006

Code	Description	Opening balance (£)	Movement (£)	Closing balance (£)
100/0010	FA – L&B	400,000	0	400,000
100/0020	FA – P&M	825,000	13,400	838,400
100/0030	FA – Cars	62,300	(10,200)	52,100
100/0110	Depreciation – L&B	(44,000)	(800)	(44,800)
100/0120	Depreciation – P&M	(374,200)	(6,700)	(380,900)
100/0130	Depreciation – Cars	(52,600)	(1,600)	(54,200)
100/0200	Trade debtors	412,371	108,611	520,982
100/0205	Prepayments	12,000	(2,000)	10,000
100/0300	Cash	108,562	12,605	121,167
100/0400	Stock – RM	44,200	8,410	52,610
100/0410	Stock – WIP	22,458	3,325	25,783
100/0420	Stock – FG	85,396	(16,752)	68,644
100/0500	Trade creditors	(636,729)	34,966	(601,763)
100/0510	Rent accrual	(6,000)	(1,000)	(7,000)
100/0520	Rates accrual	(8,500)	(1,750)	(10,250)

200/1000	Sales	2,545,312	612,658	3,157,970
200/1010	Cost of sales	1,630,587	298,652	1,929,239
300/1010	Production – labour	470,355	44,612	514,967
300/1010	Production – fuel	88,520	6,320	94,840
300/1020	Production – rates	9,000	1,000	10,000
400/1010	QC – labour	88,240	6,300	94,540
400/1050	QC – equip hire	6,420	312	6,732
600/1015	Admin – salaries	147,362	14,396	161,758
600/1062	Admin – legal fees	3,650	2,000	5,650

This extract from a trial balance shows some key features. Credit balances or movements are shown in brackets. Not obvious is the fact that the total of each column must net out to zero.

The structure, if the chart of accounts has been well thought out, puts similar accounts together for ease of understanding. Here, all balance sheet items start with 100/– – – –.

There are two types of account of particular interest:

1 **Control accounts** – where the balance can be validated by reference to another system, i.e.

   debtors ledgers = debtors control account (100/0205)
   cash book   = cash account (100/0300)
   stock control = stock accounts (100/0400 – 0420)
   creditors ledger = creditors control account (100/0500)

2 **Verifiable accounts** – at the end of the financial year, the auditors will be looking for validation and verification of *all* the closing balances, particularly in the Balance Sheet. They will want evidence relating to accounts such as:
   • fixed assets – from invoices posted in the year
   • rent accrual – verified by subsequent invoices if possible.

The audit trail

The auditors will also verify the originating causes of some transactions. For instance, in the payroll section of the accounts, they will want to track back through payments to clock cards and prove that the reported figures are right.

Outputs from the general ledger

Both the Profit and Loss Account and the Balance Sheet can be taken directly from the general ledger.

However, you will notice from the above chart of accounts that a number of useful management reports readily become available.

The first one to strike you might be expenditure by department. The report lists out the cost in each general ledger account for any given department. This produces a departmental overhead report – very useful to departmental heads, particularly if compared with budget. Most general ledgers usually hold a budget amount against each account code just for this purpose.

Secondly, the costs can be analysed by expense code – how much has been spent on overtime across all departments? This report adds together all accounts with an expense code of 2010, regardless of department.

A summary version might produce totals for related types of expenditure, either by department or a company total. This could add together all manpower costs (any expense code starting with a 4 perhaps), or all maintenance costs (expense codes ranging from 3500 to 3725). If the chart of accounts is set up initially with some forethought, much useful management information can be generated quite readily.

Not available

The general ledger should not be expected to enable managers to analyse absolutely everything. For one thing, it can only report back what has been entered into it. It does not do forecasts (although cost data could be extrapolated into the future – if we've spent £16,000 on gas in the first six months, will that become £32,000 for the full year? What is the seasonal adjustment?).

Nor is it usually the best place to do detailed analysis of numbers of sales or payroll. The chart of accounts could be set up to split out UK and export sales, it could even have a separate account code for each customer if required, but such information is probably best derived from the source system. It's the same with payroll – the general ledger isn't the place to find out if Calvin Droid received any overtime last month, the payroll system is.

By the same token, neither customer information nor product profitability come out of the general ledger, nor does anything that is quantity based rather than monetary (i.e. sales or stock units). Actually some systems can do the latter, but again, the source system (e.g. stock control) is built to answer questions like that and is the best place to access information.

The general ledger is a very good financial tool, but it has its limitations.

Key points

- The general ledger is the central collecting place for the financial transactions of all other systems.
- Transactions can be posted to the general ledger in batches or by individual detail. The posting can be by direct interface between the systems or by journal.
- Control accounts within the general ledger can be checked against source systems for debtors, creditors, cash book and stock.
- A journal is simply a form which posts values to account codes. A reversing journal swaps the values back out of the general ledger in a later period and is usually used for accruals.
- The chart of accounts represents the structure of the general ledger, with like accounts grouped together.
- A trial balance of the general ledger lists the values held in each account code.
- The key financial statements can be derived straight from the general ledger.

The origin of numbers

So, the general ledger is the place where it all comes together, rather than where things start from. It holds the value of everything, but it doesn't initiate. Most transactions are to do with buying and selling, so the costing system is a vital component in the understanding of finance.

Chapter 9 Review Questions

1 Which accounts in the general ledger are validated ˅ systems?

2 If payroll does not interface directly with the general le˅ how can the payroll transactions be posted to it?

3 What is the most common reason for using a reversing journal?

4 What will a chart of accounts reveal?

5 Which report lists the values held in the general ledger?

6 What reports can be taken directly from the general ledger?

10
costing

In this chapter you will le
- how financial informatio
  informs costing decisio
- about direct and indirec
  costs
- about variable and fixed
  costs
- about marginal and full
  costing

What's the problem?

The role of management includes making and taking decisions, and it is so much easier to get it right with all the right information.

But it's not often that managers can find out everything they'd like to know before the decision has to be made; they have to accept that there are limits to the knowledge that is available.

Managers should also be aware that the information they have may not be all that it seems, especially if it comes from Accounts!

Pick a price

Joe Thorsen, a sales manager, is faced with several decisions. He has been given information about the cost of production of fake note detectors (£12 each). He can accept all or any of three orders:

1 an order for 100 which would mean working overtime to complete.
2 an order of 100 which would keep the machines busy on Friday afternoon, otherwise they will stand idle.
3 an order for 25 of an enhanced version which will work with euros.

Joe has to decide how much to quote to each customer. The standard list price is £28.

Actually Joe is right to ponder this one. What does the £12 cost actually represent? Is it the average cost of making a detector? Is that just the cost of the materials or does it include labour as well? If so, is that labour charged at normal hourly rates?

And what about overheads, have they been taken in to account? It might make a difference to Joe's quotes.

In fact, there are different types of costing which are needed to answer different questions that may be asked in the business – you shouldn't use the same information to answer widely differing questions.

What cost includes

You would think this is a pretty obvious thing to know, but the cost of any given product can vary considerably. It all depends on how the figure is put together, which in turn depends on what you want to do with the cost once you've worked it out.

There are a number of options available as to which type of costs to include or exclude, and even within those definitions, there are different types of costs. To start with, take a look at the principal distinctions that are made between costs.

Direct v. indirect costs

This classification of costs is most commonly used in manufacturing organizations, but is increasingly applied to service-oriented functions, such as hospitals and government agencies.

Direct costs are those associated directly with the making of the product. They are usually further categorized into materials, labour and overheads. Direct materials are those that go to form the product; direct labour is the wage costs (including the employer's contributions towards pensions and national insurance) of those people who actually put the product together or make its constituent parts; direct overheads are all the other expenses directly associated with the manufacturing process, e.g. electricity for machines).

The total direct cost is sometimes called the prime cost.

This leaves indirect costs as others which are related to the production process. A similar breakdown into categories is used:
• indirect materials for consumables and maintenance materials
• indirect labour for shop-floor supervisors, product inspectors and testers
• indirect overheads such as heating and lighting.

The sum of these gives the indirect cost of production. There are, of course, other overhead costs, relating to sales and marketing, administration, accounts etc. These are, quite naturally, excluded from the cost of production and are not considered in the cost of the product.

Variable v. fixed costs

This is quite a straightforward distinction to make for a cost. If the cost goes up in proportion to the quantity produced, then it is a variable cost. If it stays the same regardless of the output, it is a fixed cost.

So the cost of tyres on a Jaguar is a variable cost – there are always five per car (including the spare). Fifty more cars means 250 more tyres. But the Managing Director's salary doesn't go up if another 50 cars are produced, so that's a fixed cost.

There has to be a fly in the ointment – there are some costs which aren't quite direct or fixed. These are stepped costs, which are fixed for most of the time, but at a certain level of production, take a jump up to another level. The cost of supervisors can come into this category.

If we only need one supervisor (at £260 per week) per eight operators and each operator can produce 100 units per week (i.e. one supervisor at £260, for every 800 units), a graph of the cost against the output quantity looks like this:

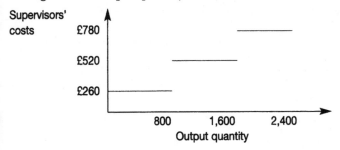

While we're on graphs, can you imagine what the graph would be for a variable and a fixed cost? What about putting them together on the same graph to show the total cost? Use this data:

Quantity	100	200	300	400
Variable costs (£)	200	400	600	800
Fixed costs (£)	500	500	500	500
Total costs (£)	700	900	1,100	1,300

The unit cost is £2 and the fixed costs will be £500, no matter what the level of production.

The graph looks like this:

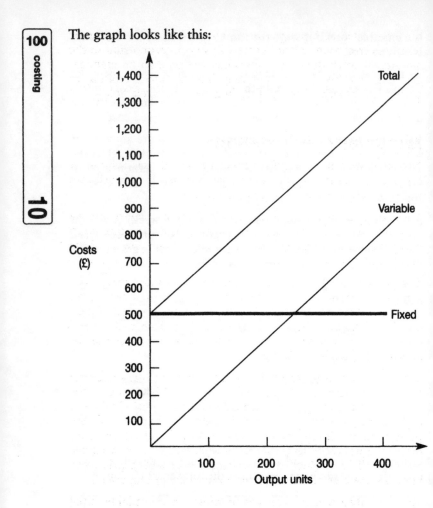

This graph comes in useful later when we look at break even analysis. The point to note for now is that the total cost per unit falls the greater the number of units that is produced, because the fixed cost is shared by more and more units of product. You can also imagine how adding stepped costs would destroy the nice smooth lines of the graph – try adding one for yourself, where for every 150 units, there is a cost of £100.

Just to tie up the relationships between direct/indirect and variable/fixed, direct costs are usually the same as variable costs and indirect ones are fixed. There are of course exceptions – direct labour is fixed to a certain point (unless workers are paid on piece rates or labour is hired and fired in the very short term), indirect maintenance costs will vary in proportion to the amount of work done on a machine, the production manager gets a salary (fixed cost) but may have a bonus relating to output (variable) and so on. But, in general, the rule holds.

Marginal v. full costing

Now that we can distinguish between different types of cost, it becomes a question of what we do with them. Or rather, do we want to include all or only some of them?

There are two costing methods, marginal and full, but before we look at the difference between them, it is important to understand why we might need one method in preference to the other in certain circumstances.

The purpose of any information system, including costing, is to give managers information that will help them make better decisions. If we are offered a contract to make and sell 10,000 compact discs for £30,000, do we accept it? That will depend on how much it costs to make them, and so we must use the appropriate cost information.

Similarly, if a company launches a new software program for the PC market, what should the selling price be? The cost of the floppy disk and the packaging plus a profit margin? Or do you include the advertising cost? Should we add in all the programming development costs? (Actually, from a pure marketing point of view, the selling price ought to be what the market will bear which is not related to the selling price, but knowing the cost at least gives us a minimum selling price.)

You must always match the type of information available to the type of decision required. So if the accountant tells you that the cost of a product is £5.50, you need to know whether that is the marginal or full cost. After we've looked at each type of cost, we will consider some examples of when to use which method.

Marginal costing

This is the simplest and least confusing method of costing, although it has its limitations.

To clarify a point, the marginal cost is all the variable costs of production (the direct costs which are nearly always variable) and those overheads related to production which are variable in relation to output.

If the marginal cost is the same as the direct and variable indirect costs, working out the cost per unit is simple.

Let us take as an example a company that makes car batteries.

In a four-week period, our car battery manufacturer produces, for the moment, just one type of battery – a 12-volt model. Here are the costs and the production figures:

Production costs of making 12v batteries	
	£
Variable:	
Materials	1,600
Labour	1,000
Expenses	500
Variable overheads	200
Total variable	3,300
Quantity (units)	400

So the marginal cost is the variable costs divided by the output:

£3,300 / 400 = £8.25 per unit.

Management might make some assumptions and use this figure to calculate that to make another 100 batteries would add to the costs 100 × £8.25 = £825. In practice this estimate would probably not be far wrong, but managers would have to bear in mind questions such as:
- Would the extra output require premium overtime working?
- Would any stepped costs jump to the next level at an output of 500 units?
- Would there be any impact on non-variable costs not included in the £8.25 (i.e. additional maintenance costs)?

None of these points are taken into account when marginal costing is used.

Full costing

This is so called because it includes the full production costs when calculating the unit cost of the product. It is also called absorption costing, since all the product costs are absorbed into the unit cost of production.

Now, let's go back to our car battery manufacturer and add some overhead costs information:

	£
Variable:	
Materials	1,600
Labour	1,000
Expenses	500
Variable overheads	200
Total variable	3,300
Fixed production costs:	
Materials	500
Labour	900
Expenses	600
Total fixed	2,000
Quantity (units)	400

The marginal cost is unchanged at £8.25. The full cost of the total of all production costs (variable and fixed) incurred by the company divided by the output:

$$(3,300 + 2,000) / 400 = £13.25$$

Now doesn't that make a difference? Would you willingly sell a battery for £12 now you know that? The difference is that we have now set all other costs against that product. If we don't receive at least £13.25 for each of those 400 batteries produced, the company will not make a contribution to other (non-production) overheads.

But what if we produce 500 batteries? The variable costs will, by definition, change in line with output and the fixed costs must stay the same. The outcome is:

	£
Variable:	
Materials	2,000
Labour	1,250
Expenses	625
Variable overheads	250
Total variable	4,125
Fixed production costs:	
Materials	500
Labour	900
Expenses	600
Production fixed	2,000
Quantity (units)	500

The marginal cost stays the same (as it must):

> 4,125 / 500 = £8.25

but the full cost falls:

> (4,125 + 2,000) / 500 = £12.25.

This is because we have spread the fixed costs of the company over more units, and the fixed component of the full cost has gone from to £5 to £4. So the more we make, the lower the cost!

Note this depends very heavily upon the assumption that fixed costs do remain absolutely fixed. If we get carried away with reducing the full cost of unit production by increasing production, until the full cost almost equals the marginal cost, we would outstrip current capacity and require another factory, incurring a whole new batch of fixed costs! It's these stepped costs which can catch you out, because they look fixed – but only until a certain threshold of production is reached.

Making a second product

In the real world, there aren't many companies that make just one version of one product without any variations. This multiplicity of product offerings makes costing a little trickier, although the principles used so far hold good.

Using marginal costing, let's look at the battery manufacturer again, with an additional product, a 16-volt model, which we will assume runs on a separate production line:

	12v	16v	Total
	£	£	£
Variable:			
Materials	1,000	1,000	2,000
Labour	1,600	600	2,200
Expenses	500	300	800
Variable overheads	200	300	500
Total variable	3,300	2,200	5,500
Quantity (units)	400	200	

The marginal cost of the products are:
- 12v – £8.25
- 16v – £11.00 (2,200 / 200).

Simple enough, so let's look at the full cost.

One problem encountered straight away is that there are fixed costs to include in the unit costs of production, but we have two products. So how do we share those costs between them? The fixed costs are not directly related to the production of any particular product, so on what basis should the costs be allocated? There are, as ever, a number of alternatives:

1 **50/50** – would that be fair? There were only 200 16-volt batteries produced against 400 of the 12v model. Then again why not? What difference does it make to supervisors' costs how many of each were produced? Not a jot.
2 **By quantity produced** – two-thirds of the fixed costs should be allocated to the 12v model by virtue of it making up two-thirds of the total units.
3 **By labour hours** – the direct labour cost of the two products is:

> 12v   £1,600
> 16v   £600

Assuming the same grade (and hourly rate of pay) of labour is used for each, then 12v batteries have taken more than two-and-a-half times longer to make than 16v batteries (the labour cost is two-and-a-half times greater; £1600 compared with £600). So shouldn't the 12v battery bear two-and-a-half times more of the fixed costs?

Let's see what difference each alternative method of overhead cost allocation makes to the full costs, keeping total production fixed costs as before (£2,000 for production) and introducing £2,500 of other company overheads (selling and administration costs etc.).

	1 50/50	2 Output	3 Labour
12v:			
Marginal (£)	8.25	8.25	8.25
Fixed (£)	2.50	3.33	3.64
Total (£)	10.75	11.58	11.89
16v:			
Marginal (£)	11.00	11.00	11.00
Fixed (£)	5.00	3.33	2.73
Total (£)	26.00	14.33	13.73

So – you can check the numbers – the allocation of the fixed cost (£2,000) to each product under the different methods is:

	12v	**16v**
1 50/50	£1,000	£1,000
2 Output	£1,333	£667
3 Labour	£1,455	£545

Note that even when these different full costs are calculated, the costs of the company do not change. All these methods do is spread the cost round in different ways. Only three methods of allocation are demonstrated here; there are many more that could be used – machine hours used, direct wages, prime cost, all sorts of ratios – but they all do the same thing, just move the cost from one side to another. The total doesn't change. You may realize that this means, with judicious allocation of overheads, one product can be made to appear cheaper to produce than others, but literally at the expense of those others.

Also, notice that depending on which method of allocation is used, the overhead burden of 12v batteries can be more, the same or less than that of 16v ones!

Which way is best? That's a choice for the individual user, depending on what she wants to do with the information. One thing though, in full costing, the fixed element of the cost is also referred to as the overhead recovery rate. This is a key number, because when multiplied by the production output units, it gives a sum that recovers the overheads.

In the example, we have used quantities of 400 (12v) and 200 (16v) to give recovery rates of £3.64 and £2.73 respectively, under the labour rate allocation. What if, next month, 500 and 400 units are produced?

The marginal costs are variable, so they should stay in line at £8.25 and £11. And if production overheads are fixed, they should be the same at £2,000.

But what will we have 'recovered'?
        12v: 500 × £3.64 = £1,820
        16v: 400 × £2.73 = £<u>1,092</u>
        Total   £2,912

This is what the accountant will call an over recovery of £912 (£2,912 – £2,000). An under recovery occurs when overhead expenditure is higher than the amount 'recovered' by production output.

This under or over recovery can be put straight into the Profit and Loss Account to increase or decrease overheads for the period. Alternatively, it can be used to adjust the stock value in the Balance Sheet, implicitly recognizing that the recovery rate was not the true and accurate one needed when the real results became available.

Note that overhead recovery is based on production quantities, not sales.

Using the information

The cost, marginal or full, calculated for a unit of production can be used to value the stock and consequently, the cost of product sold. Obviously using full costing gives a higher stock value and a higher cost of sales, but the cost of overheads deducted as expenses in the Profit and Loss Account is lower because of the overhead recovery factor.

The car battery manufacturer has the following results for the period:

	12v	16v	Total
Units – production	400	200	
– sales	£300	£150	
Sales revenue	£6,000	£3,750	£9,750
Production costs	**£**	**£**	**£**
Variable:			
Materials	1,600	1,000	2,600
Labour	1,000	600	1,600
Expenses	500	300	800
Variable overheads	200	300	500
Total variable	<u>3,300</u>	<u>2,200</u>	<u>5,500</u>
Overheads:			
Production fixed	2,000		
R&D	500		
Sales and marketing	1,200		
Administration	800		

There are no opening stocks and the company uses labour hours to determine the allocation of fixed overheads to products when it uses the full costing method.

To see the difference in using marginal and full costing methods, we need first to know the unit costs of production. The company uses labour hours to determine the allocation of fixed overheads to products. Fortunately we've already done this.

	12v	**16v**
Marginal	£8.25	£11.00
Full	£11.89	£13.73

With marginal costing, the stock and cost of sales are:

12 volts

	Units	Cost (£)/unit	Cost (£)
Produced	400	8.25	3,300
Sold	(300)	8.25	(2,475)
Closing stock	100	8.25	825

16 volts

	Units	Cost (£)/unit	Cost (£)
Produced	200	11.00	2,200
Sold	(150)	11.00	(1,650)
Closing stock	50	11.00	550
Total closing stock			1,375
Total cost of sales			4,125

Using full costing, the stock and cost of sales are:

12 volts

	Units	Cost (£)/unit	Cost (£)
Produced	400	11.89	4,756
Sold	(300)	11.89	(3,567)
Closing stock	100	11.89	1,189

16 volts

	Units	Cost (£)/unit	Cost (£)
Produced	200	13.73	2,746
Sold	(150)	13.73	(2,060)
Closing stock	50	13.73	687
Total closing stock			1,876
Total cost of sales			5,627
Overheads recovered	(400 × £3.64 + 200 × £2.73)		2,002

The stock value under full costing is higher because it has an element of overhead recovery included.

Now put the Profit and Loss Account together.

	Marginal £	Full £
Sales	9,750	9,750
Cost of sales	4,125	5,627
Margin	5,625	4,123
Overheads:		
Production fixed	2,000	2,000
R&D	500	500
Sales and Marketing	1,200	1,200
Administration	800	800
Less recovered	–	(2,002)
Total overheads	4,500	2,498
Profit	1,125	1,625

There is a £500 difference in the profit, just because we used a different method of costing! It's nothing to do with selling or operational activities, the actual transactions are the same.

Where's the difference? It's in the closing stock figures.

To prove it,

	Closing stock (units)	Overhead recovery rate (£/unit)	Overheads in stock
12v	100	3.64	364
16v	50	2.73	136
Total			500

Doesn't it all balance out beautifully?

So which to use?

If the battery company is offered a contract to supply fifty 12-volt batteries over and above the 300 sold already, should it accept a price of £12 per battery?

Marginal costing would indicate yes. Since the cost is £8.25 there is a clear contribution to overheads of 50 × £2.75 = £137.50. Since overheads are fixed anyway, this will simply increase the profits by £137.50 or to use the accounting jargon, it will simply 'fall through to the bottom line'.

With full costing at £11.89 per battery, are you tempted to turn the offer down? Accepting the contract will reduce profits by £44.50 (50 × (£11 – £11.89)). You would appear to be right to refuse, because the 3,000 units need to be sold at an average of £11.89 each just to break even.

Common sense would, hopefully, allow you to judge that a good transaction is a good transaction, no matter what the costing method used. The reason the fixed cost makes the offer look a poor one is because some of the fixed overhead expenditure has not been taken into the Profit and Loss Account yet – it's 'buried' in the stock value. But when that stock is sold later, the overheads recovery element of the stock will come out in the cost of sales figure, reducing the profits.

Over time (when all stocks are sold), the profits of the firm will be the same whether marginal or full costing is used. The following example demonstrates this.

	Marginal			**Full**		
	Month 1	*Month 2*	*Total*	*Month 1*	*Month 2*	*Total*
Units – production	400	400	800	400	400	800
– sales	300	500	800	300	500	800
Revenue (£20/unit)	6,000	10,000	16,000	6,000	10,000	16,000
Production costs:	£	£	£	£	£	£
Materials, labour, expenses variable						
overheads	3,300	3,300	6,600	3,300	3,300	6,600
Fixed costs:						
Production	2,000	2,000	4,000	2,000	2,000	4,000
Other	2,500	2,500	5,000	2,500	2,500	5,000
Stocks and cost of sales						
		Units	*Cost*	*Value*	*Units*	*Cost*
Value						
Month 1 production	400	8.25	3,300	400	13.25	5,300
– sold	(300)	8.25	2.475	(300)	13.25	3.975
Closing stock	100	8.25	825	100	13.25	1,325
Month 2 production	400	8.25	3,300	400	13.25	5,300
– sold	(500)	8.25	(4,125)	(500)	13.25	(6,625)

Profit and Loss Account

Total	Month 1	Month 2	Total	Month 1	Month 2
Sales revenue	6,000	10,000	16,000	6,000	10,000	16,000
Cost of sales	2,475	4,125	6,600	3,975	6,625	10,600
Gross margin	3,525	5,875	9,400	2,025	3,375	5,400
Overheads:						
– Production	2,000	2,000	4,000	2,000	2,000	4,000
less recovered	–	–	–	(2,000)	(2,000)	(4,000)
plus other	2,500	2,500	5,000	2,500	2,500	5,000
Profit	(975)	1,375	400	(475)	875	400

Although the total over the two periods is the same regardless of the method chosen, the reason for the difference in Month 1 is the production overheads. In marginal costing, they are written off (deducted from profit) in the month in which they occur. In full costing, the production overheads aren't deducted until the product which incurred the cost is sold.

Having now banished the mystery behind what a cost is or might be, you are now in a position to bandy words about with the cost accountant (who calculates these things) and ask pertinent questions such as:
• Is this the marginal cost of production or does it include an element of overheads?
• Are we already in a position of over recovery on overheads so I can price this special contract a little lower?
• Why does product A have a higher cost than B when they are very similar items? Does B have more overheads arbitrarily allocated to it? On what basis? Is that a fair and reasonable way of allocating the costs?

Costing and the pricing decision

There often seems to be some confusion in managers' minds as to the relationship between what a product actually costs to make and how much it should be sold for.

We have already seen that making a product can be shown to cost different amounts, depending on the costing system used. Managers from different functions may try to extrapolate the calculated cost into a selling price using various levels of mark-up, but they misunderstand the distinction between the cost and the selling price.

According to marketing and economic theory, the selling price of a product has no relationship with its cost at all – the selling price should simply be what the customer is prepared to pay for it. The only relevance of the cost is that, if the price customers want to pay is below the cost of making a product, perhaps it is time to stop production.

Variations – incremental and contract

Incremental costing

There is a little confusion over the distinction between marginal and incremental costing.

In accounting speak, the distinction is made in this way – *marginal costing* is the equivalent of the variable costs of production while *incremental costing* is the cost of producing one more unit. They are not necessarily the same thing. It is rare for incremental costing to be used in commercial decision making, partly because the information available to calculate it is not always accurate and it always produces a lower figure than marginal costing. To err on the safe side, managers stick with the higher marginal cost.

Contract costing

Contract costing features more frequently, particularly in businesses that do contract work like construction. In this type of activity, many costs can be specifically identified with a particular project and charged to it, such as power and utilities costs relating to the site. In a manufacturing operation these would be indirect costs, but if they can be recognized as being caused solely by the contract's activities, they can be charged fully to it.

There would also be some indirect costs (head office charges etc.), but these would be relatively small compared with the costs clearly identifiable as being directly attributed to the contract.

There are other variations – process, job and batch costing – which use the same principles as the other methods, but generally have a slightly different approach to defining and allocating costs.

Key points
- Direct costs arise from the making of the product and can be analysed into labour, materials and overheads. The total direct cost is also known as the prime cost.
- Indirect costs are also related to the production process, but as a service or support to it.
- Variable costs are proportional to the amount produced. Fixed costs remain unchanged (in the short term). Stepped costs stay fixed until a certain level of production is attained, then increase to a higher fixed amount.
- Marginal costing calculates the cost of production by dividing the total variable costs by the number of items produced.
- Full, or absorption costing, takes into account the fixed production costs, by calculating an overhead recovery element. The total cost of production is the variable and fixed costs added together – dividing by the output quantity gives the full cost per unit.
- If there is more than one product being made, the fixed costs have to be allocated to them using one method or another. Whichever method is chosen, it does not reduce the total costs; it just passes them back to the products in differing amounts.

Moving the goalposts

And just when you think you've got a complete understanding, the cost accountant will say, 'In reality, because we don't know what the actual costs are until after the end of the accounting period, and we need to have some costs to use until we get the actuals, we'll have to use standard costing.' See Chapter 11!

Chapter 10 Review Questions

1 Which of these costs of making castings are direct or indirect:
   a a lathe operator's wages?
   b his supervisor's salary?
   c maintenance costs of the lathe?
   d the metal blocks used to make the product?
   e the running costs of the forklift truck that carries material from and to stores?

2 Differentiate between variable, fixed and stepped costs.

3 What is the difference between marginal and full costing? Which elements are included only in the latter?

4 How is the overhead recovery rate derived for a single product?

5 What methods can be used to allocate fixed costs over a number of products?

6 How should the selling price of a product be set in relation to its cost?

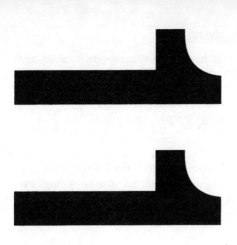

standard costing

In this chapter you will learn
- why standard costing is used
- how a standard costing is obtained
- about standard costing and budgets

What's the problem?

In Chapter 3 we looked at how the value of stock could vary depending on the method used, e.g. FIFO, LIFO or average cost. In each purchase transaction that we looked at there, the value per unit was based upon the purchase price.

If there are literally hundreds or even thousands of purchases during each period, calculating the average cost, or keeping track of the FIFO/LIFO stock gets very tricky. It also means you have to wait for the actual numbers from the transactions to be available before the calculations can be made. Being ever inventive, and preferring an easy life, accountants have devised another piece of financial wizardry – standard costing.

Not a real cost

The standard cost of a product is a predetermined value assigned to it, based on simple rules. However, the rules are flexible, in that there are a considerable number of options and methods that can be applied! Standard price can be a steady and useful figure in a changing world of inflation, price increases, currency fluctuations and competing suppliers with ever improving offers.

So to keep things simple, a product has a standard cost which doesn't change that often, because it is a cost applied to that product all the time, regardless of what the real cost of the product is. The advantages of using standard cost are:
- you know what it is this week and next
- you don't have to spend all day trying to work out what the real cost is, when prices are changing and stock is flowing in and out
- it can be useful for some types of decisions (e.g. setting minimum prices)
- by reporting the significant differences between actual and standard costs (variances), management time and effort can be concentrated on problem areas.

The downside includes:
- the standard cost may not be that close to the real cost
- consequently, stock values may be under- or overstated
- it could be misleading if used for certain types of decisions (e.g. contract pricing).

What's wrong with actual data?

Nothing at all! In fact, it must be actual results that are used in compiling the published figures, the Profit and Loss Account and the Balance Sheet.

Using standards for operational activities gives rise to variances when they are compared with actual figures. These variances can then indicate to management where their time and energies ought to be devoted. This principle is called management by exception – only the problem areas are highlighted, meaning that management don't have to expend effort looking after things that are working perfectly well.

Marginal or full costing?

Like the actual costs shown in Chapter 10, standard costs can be based on marginal or full costing principles. The choice of method depends on what the information is to be used for, but always find out which method is being used when costs are quoted. We've already seen that it can make quite a difference.

So what is a standard cost?

A standard cost is a benchmark cost given to a product. The standard cost for a finished good (one that is to be sold) is derived from at least one, and usually a second, source of information.

The first is a bill of materials (BOM). This is a list of all the component parts that go into making the finished item. Some of the components themselves may be made up of sub-components. Diagrammatically, the BOM may start looking like this:

	Sewing machine	
Level 0		
Level 1	Motor	Housing	Cable
Level 2	Transformer	Needle	Plug
	Gearing	Base	Wiring
	.	.	.
	.	.	.
	.	.	.

Each component has a material standard cost and the sum of their material standard costs is the material standard cost of the finished product. If the basis for standard costs is materials only, then that's all there is to it.

The standard materials cost for the lowest level of product is based on a standard purchase price, because these products must be bought in from external suppliers. (If they are not bought in, they must be, by definition, manufactured. So then they would have their own BOM, with a lower level of bought-in materials.) Similarly, any products which are bought for resale without any further processing will have a standard cost which comprises only of a material standard cost which is based on its purchase price.

However, most companies like to reflect some of the costs of production in their product costs. This can include direct labour plus direct production expenses (plus fixed production costs for full costing only).

In standard costing, that's where routing comes in. Routing is simply identifying what process the finished good and its component parts must go through to make the completed item. Using the sewing machine as an example again, the following operations might occur:
• welding of casing
• plating the casing
• assembly of motor
• final assembly
• testing.

Now these operations can be broken down into smaller tasks which can be timed, e.g. mount motor in casing, screw casing to body – 4 minutes 20 seconds.

Given that timing and a standard rate of pay for a shop floor operative, a labour cost can be calculated:

4 mins 20 sec @ £5.40/hour = 39 pence.

So 39p is added to the cost of each product that goes through this particular process.

Working out a standard

Establishing a bill of materials (the material content of made-up products) is a simple enough exercise – a can of pop includes a certain amount of metal in the can and required amounts of ingredients to make the drink. It's also possible to know the number of screws needed to build a particular type of aeroplane if that level of detail is required and recorded. But a few extra pence in something costing several million pounds is neither here nor there, so a few extra screws may be relatively insignificant.

Setting up the routing can be a little more complicated. The path a given item takes through the factory is easy to find out – it can be followed round physically, noting what happens where. Time and motion specialists can determine how long each activity takes and the number of units processed in that time at that stage. Actually, the operators themselves can do the same analysis much cheaper, provided you're prepared to rely on their findings!

Once the time taken per unit is known at each stage of the process, the cost accountant adds the last bit of necessary information – the total cost involved in completing that task. It will be split into two levels – labour and overheads.

For instance, a final assembly operation, in which all the component parts are put together, ought to complete six products in an hour. There are two people on the production line who normally get paid £6.80 per hour and they usually work a 35-hour week for 48 weeks of the year (they get four weeks' holiday). In addition, they need to use other materials (solder, electricity, etc.) which should have a total cost of £4,032 per year.

The labour and material cost assigned to the product for this assembly operation is calculated like this:

Labour	Cost per hour: 2 × 4.80 = £13.60	
	Units per hour	6
	Labour cost per unit	= £2.27
Material	Annual cost	£4,032
	Annual production	10,080 (6 × 35 × 48)
	Material cost per unit	= 40p

So the marginal cost for this stage is £2.67 per unit.

But, you say, this is the *actual* cost. Where does standard costing come into it?

Notice the paragraph above the box had a few *shoulds* and *oughts* in it – indicating what *should* happen in standard conditions. In practice, the operators may get paid more because of overtime or receive a pay increase during the year. They might produce an average of 6.4 units per hour over the year, and incur costs of £4,212 during that same time.

But to start with, we need a basis of comparison, a benchmark – in fact, a standard. The standard cost is derived from standard rates of pay, standard times of operations, standard patterns of expenditure, standard quantities of production. None of these standards may actually become reality and, when they don't, the differences between actual events and the expected standard results produce variances. These variances are useful in managing a company and are analysed in more detail later.

Setting the standard

There are three bases for setting standards, although one of them is not used much in practice.

1 **Ideal** – this uses figues for all activities and costs as they would be under the best conditions. Employees and machines work steadily away, producing maximum output. There is no material wastage, and direct production overheads run at the minimum required. Even fixed production overheads are kept as low as possible.
2 **Expected** – this takes a more realistic view of what's likely to go on in the production process. People will not perform at their maximum all the time, there will be wastage and damage of material, expenses will vary, both variable and fixed. But we can set a standard based on what we *expect* to happen under normal circumstances.
3 **Basic** – these are long-term standards, hardly ever changed and the variances between these and actuals give an indication of the changes in the real world over time. They are not much use for management application in the shorter term.

The use of budgets in setting standards

The use of budgets as standards is a very common practice. After all, if you reckon that in the coming budget year, you need to manufacture 120,000 sun lamps, then that is obviously what you plan to do at the start of the year. Associated with that budgeted quantity will be budgeted production costs.

In all likelihood these will not be very detailed; not down to the individual level of Harry Biggs and Joanne Jones in Plating, who are budgeted to be paid £10,000 plus £2,000 overtime and Samantha Harris, the Plating supervisor, £15,000. More likely there will be a labour budget for the Plating operation as a whole and an expenses one too, covering the cost of consumables and utilities.

Yet we can use the budget data to set the standard costs:

Production quantity = 120,000 sun lamps		
Plating costs:		
Labour	– direct	£24,000
	– indirect	£15,000
Overheads	– direct	£60,000
	– indirect	£33,000
This gives rise to standard costs of:		
		£
Marginal costs	– direct labour	0.20
	– direct overheads	0.50
Total marginal standard cost		0.70
Overhead recovery rate		0.40

There will be budgets for all the activities required to produce sun lamps – perhaps some different operations will be merged for the sake of the production budget. For instance, the operations of final assembly and inspection may all take place in the same department and, from the budget point of view, there may be only one set of costs. Operationally, they may be seen as separate and distinct activities. If so desired there could be a nominal split of the budget, purely for standard costing purposes, to help determine the appropriate cost of items passing through the process.

The sum of all the standard costs of all the budgeted operations gives the total standard cost for the product. The problems of allocating shared costs or fixed production costs not specific to any particular operation remain the same as for the actual full costing method discussed in Chapter 10 – some allocation method is required and whichever one is chosen can move the fixed overhead element of the standard cost from one product to another.

When to change the standards

Particularly if they are based on the budget, standard costs tend to stay the same for the whole of the accounting year. This will usually mean that actual costs are quite different from standard ones towards the end of the year, due to price rises and unexpected (unbudgeted) circumstances like lost customers (affecting budget and standard quantities) and machine breakdowns.

It may be that, during the year, the difference between the standard and the actual costs becomes so great that the standards are meaningless and dangerous to use in decision making. If a manager can no longer assume that standard costs are pretty close to the real thing, what is the point of having the standard costs? None whatsoever, so change them.

One consequence of changing the standard costs is the resulting change in stocks and profitability. Usually standard costs have to increase to catch up with actual costs. If we have 5,000 sun lamps in stock at the end of December and the standard cost is raised from £40 to £45, the stock is suddenly revalued by £25,000.

Suddenly the company has more assets to the value of £25,000 – an instant windfall for doing absolutely nothing. Of course, this isn't in real money, just book figures or a paper profit. The cost of sales in the future will be higher, because the unit cost is now £5 more, but if the adjustment is timed right (say at a financial year end), the reported figures can be made to look a little better – at least until the following months, when the margin (the difference between sales and the cost of sales) comes down, since the product now appears more expensive.

Getting actual costs

In many manufacturing companies where standard costing is applied, there may be some recording of actual results on the shop floor. These are usually focused on labour and machine time, since expenses for materials and overheads are recorded in the general ledger and can be analysed there.

A common practice is to set up a job card for each product, detailing its bill of materials and the routing it takes through various stages of the production process, including labour and machine times. When a batch of finished goods is required, a works order is raised, stating how many are required and by when.

With the works order is a routing card, starting with the first operation required. The operator responsible fills in the start and finish times of the task, together with the quantity produced, before passing the batch along to whoever carries out the next operation.

And so it goes on, throughout the process, until the goods are finally complete. The routing card now carries the full actual time needed to make the product, which can be compared with the standard.

Key points

- Standard costs are not the same as the real actual costs. They are predetermined costs which act as a benchmark for calculating the value of stocks and the cost of sales.
- Items which are simply bought in from outside suppliers can be given a standard cost initially based on the purchase price.
- Manufactured items have a bill of materials stating how much of which materials it uses to make the item. There will also be a routing card associated with the item, which states the processes that the item goes through in manufacturing and how long each stage takes. This gives rise to further direct costs attached to the item.
- Marginal or full costing principles can be applied to standard costing.
- Budgets can be used as the basis of the standards. The standards can also be set in the expectation of ideal, expected or basic conditions, although expected is the most common approach.
- Problems may arise if standards vary too much from actual results. Management information may become inaccurate, so the standards have to be updated periodically.

And so ...

Standard costs are there to make life a little simpler. They are there as a steady ship in a sea of changing activities and prices. Decisions can be made on the basis of standard costs, without having to wait for the real results to become apparent.

What happens when actual costs in the real world differ from the standards or budget is the subject of the next chapter on variance analysis.

Chapter 11 Review Questions

1 Why use standard costs instead of actual costs?
2 What is the basis for setting the standard cost for
   a a bought-in item?
   b a manufactured item?
3 What is a bill of materials?
4 What is a routing?
5 When should standards be changed?

12 variance analysis

In this chapter you will learn
- about variances and standard costing
- about the key variances used in management accounting
- how variances affect sales
- how to report variances

Getting back to reality

Standards all are very well, but the activities of the company are measured by real numbers, not by what ought to have happened. The difference between the standards and the actual results are variances, and this is probably the most mathematical part of accounting.

That said, the formula for a variance is usually quite simple, especially at the top level – it's just the standard less the actual value.

However, to help determine the root causes behind the differences it is necessary to break down the higher level variances into their component parts – the topic of variance analysis.

Practical application

Variance analysis can be very useful in helping managers run the company. It can also be used too much, flooding management with tidal waves of information.

For that reason, analysis in practice is usually restricted to a few key variances, although there are others that can be calculated theoretically.

New terminology also arises in variance analysis – the variances are deemed to be either favourable or adverse, their definitions being self-evident.

The best way to understand variances is to work some out and interpret what they mean.

Materials variances

Suppose the standard cost for making a batch of 100 litres of fruit juice is made up of:

	Quantity	Price	Cost/batch (£)
Concentrate	24 litres	0.80 (£/litre)	19.20
Sugar	2 kg	1.60 (£/kg)	3.20
Water	76 litres	0.02 (£/litre)	1.52

It doesn't matter whether these are ideal, expected or basic standards – these are the numbers that the company uses, against which actual results will be compared.

The total standard material cost is £23.92 per batch. In September, the following costs and quantities were incurred in production of 20,000 litres (200 batches) of fruit juice:

Concentrate	4,800 litres costing £4,080
Sugar	430 kg costing £645
Water	15,800 litres costing £316.

Using common sense, there could be two reasons why any given material input does not come out exactly as standard:

1 in buying the material, we paid more or less than standard
2 in the production process, we used more or less than standard.

The first reason is called the materials price variance and the second is the materials usage variance. Together they add to the total materials variance for each material. For each material, we will calculate the total variance then split it down into the price and usage variances.

Concentrate

Standard material cost for 200 batches would be:

$200 \times 24 \times 80p$	= £3,840
Actual	= £4,080
Total material variance	= £240 adverse

That makes this quantity of fruit juice cost £240 more than would have been expected according to the standards. Was it because of the cost of the concentrate or the amount used?

Price variance

The formula is:

actual production × (standard price – actual price)

$4,800 \times (0.80 - 0.85) = £240$ adverse

Usage variance

This is calculated by:

standard price × (standard quantity – actual quantity)

$0.80 \times (4,800 - 4,800) = $ nil

So it was all down to the cost of the concentrate. Now do the same for sugar.

> Standard material cost = 200 × 2 kg × 1.60 = £640
> Actual cost   = £645
> **Total materials variance**   =   £5 adverse

To be just £5 adrift from standard may not seem a lot, but it may hide something significant.

> **Price variance:**   430 × (1.60 – 1.50)   = £43 favourable
> **Usage variance:** 1.60 × (400 – 430)   = £48 adverse

So the £5 total material variance was made up of two much larger variances that almost cancelled each other out. This is a point to be aware of – a poor result in part of the process may be hidden by an equally good result elsewhere. Unless the poor performance is identified, it is unlikely to be rectified.

Finally, let's do the calculations for water.

> **Total materials variance**   = £12 adverse
> **Price variance**   = nil
> **Usage variance**   = £12 adverse

All in the usage this time – it took 600 litres more than standard to make the batch.

Now you can add all the different types of variance from all three materials to produce a total materials variance:

> **Total materials variance**   = £257 adverse
> **Total materials price variance**   = £48 adverse
> **Total materials usage variance**   = £209 adverse

This is easy to check – for 200 batches of production, the materials cost should be 200 × £23.92 = £4,784. The actual cost is £4,080 + £645 + £316 = £5,041 – a difference of £257.

It's one thing to know what the variances are, but this doesn't reveal what caused them. The total variance is split into price and usage to indicate where the reason might lie, but that isn't the end of it. With price, why did we pay more for the concentrate? Was there a change of supplier? A movement in currency rates? Did we buy a smaller quantity and lose a bulk buy discount?

Similarly with the usage variance, the numbers do not tell what caused it. Inefficient production? Poor quality product? Simple wastage?

There can be a connection between the causes of the price and usage variances. For instance, buying cheaper, lower quality materials will give a favourable price variance, but may cause production problems leading to an unfavourable usage variance. Only if the total of the two is still favourable will the deal have been worth it (ignoring the problems it caused the production manager!).

Direct labour variance

The principle is similar for the direct labour variance. It can be split into two, a rate variance and an efficiency variance.

Producing fruit juice again, the standard labour cost per batch of 100 litres is 40 minutes at £6.00 per hour = £4.00. In that same September, the 200 batches produced took 140 hours at a labour cost of £847. Also the labour rate in that department is actually £6.05 per hour.

If you think of the rate variance as akin to the materials price variance and the efficiency variance as a materials usage one, the formula are pretty much the same.

Standard labour cost = 200 × £4 = £800
Actual labour cost   = £847
Total labour variance   = (£47)

(Note that adverse variances can also be shown in brackets.)

Labour rate variance =
actual production hours × (standard rate – actual rate)
= 140 × (£6 – £6.05) = (£7)

> **Labour efficiency variance** =
> standard labour rate × (standard production hours – actual hours)
> = £6 × (133.33 – 140) = (£40).

So the deviation in labour costs is due to poor efficiency rather than pay rates. However, before storming over to the supervisor and berating her for letting the operators stand idle, consider whether the standards are properly set. Are they ideal standards or do they allow for some downtime? Do they ask for unreasonable standards of performance?

Indeed if variances are consistently adrift in either direction, favourable or adverse, perhaps they ought to be reviewed to bring them more into line with what is actually going on. Like budgets, sometimes it's the benchmark that's wrong, not the actuals.

The materials and labour variances are the key ones most often used. However, a firm with a range of products requiring a huge number of materials can have a stream of variances. But the principle of the calculation remains the same, it's just that there might be more of them. In the case of such a firm, two things will probably happen:

1 only a summary level of variances will be calculated initially
2 only those of significant size will be reported.

However, if any variance causes concern, it can be analysed in more detail to identify the originating cause. This would only be done upon request, since there is no benefit in churning out lots of numbers which are never used.

Overheads aren't quite the same

As we have seen other variances can be calculated in a similar way, but aren't as widely used. Part of the reason is that there is not often, in practice, a real direct relationship between overheads, direct or fixed, and the standards used. The standards implicitly assume a linear relationship between quantity and cost where none may actually exist.

Mathematically a difference can be explained, but in the real world, does producing an extra 10% units add 10% to the consumption of power? Do consumables rise by 10%? Reality ignores what is supposed to happen according to the theoretical standards.

Management control of overheads tends to be based on absolute figures, with an eye to the production level, but if the emphasis is on keeping overhead costs down, then variances are likely to be favourable anyway.

To complete the picture, the variances relating to overheads are now presented. Note that in these examples, and the previous ones, actual prices/rates are never used in the calculation of a variance except in the price/rate variance which is calculated first. After that, it's always based on standard price/rate.

Overhead variance analysis

The problem with setting standards relating to overheads has already been discussed. But to calculate a variance, there has to be some basis of allocation of the costs to the products (if it cannot be done directly) usually in relation to the machine or labour hours required.

This also applies when full costing is used and fixed production overheads are apportioned.

If there were two products involved and the overheads could not be directly attributed to either of them specifically, they could be apportioned on the basis of machine or labour hours required to make the budgeted production quantity, as shown below.

	Product A	Product B
Production (units)	40,000	50,000
Machine hours/unit	2.5	4.0
Machine hours required	80,000	200,000
Production overheads:		
Variable £42,000		
Fixed £70,000		
Recovery rate/machine hour:		
Variable £0.15 = £42,000/(80,000 + 200,000)		
Fixed £0.25		
Allocation of production overheads (apportioned on machine hours required):		
Variable	£12,000	£30,000
Fixed	£20,000	£50,000

Our fruit juice maker only has the one product and has based its standard costing on the annual budget. For an annual production of 300,000 litres (3,000 batches), the production overheads are budgeted in total at
• Variable £30,000
• Fixed £48,000.

Because there is only the one product made, the costs can be allocated directly to the number of litres produced:
• Variable overhead recovery rate £10 per batch
• Fixed overhead recovery rate £16 per batch.

This is simply dividing the cost by the production volume. However, to be able to calculate the overhead variances – which uses labour or machine hours – we need to know the *hourly* recovery rate. Because it takes 40 minutes to make a batch, converting the batch recovery rates into recovery rates per hour is simple:
• Variable overhead recovery rate = £15 per batch (£10 × 60/40)
• Fixed overhead recovery rate = £24 per batch (£16 × 60/40)

Variable overhead variances

In September, the actual expenditure on variable overheads was £2,200 for a production of 200 batches. Actual production labour hours were 140.

For production of 200 batches, it should have taken 133.33 hours (at 40 minutes per batch) and variable overheads ought to have been, according to the standard, 133.33 × £15 = £2,000. The overspend of £200 is an adverse total variable overhead variance. It can be analysed further (this shows why we need the hourly version of the overhead recovery):

Variable overhead expenditure variance =
(actual hours at the standard recovery rate) – (actual variable overheads) = (140 × £15) – £2,200 = (£100)

Variable overhead efficiency variance =
(standard hours at the standard rate) – (actual hours at the standard rate) = (133.33 × £15) – (140 × £15) = (£100)

The first variance means that the manufacturer was actually spending more per hour of production on variable overheads. The second that the company spent longer making the production volume than was set in the standard.

When put in that sort of English, instead of formula and accounting language, it is easier to think of reasons why the variances might have arisen. The efficiency variance is obviously tied to the labour efficiency variance, since they both rely on how many labour hours production took against what it ought to have taken. Expenditure variance indicates that costs were higher than standard expectations. In this instance, the total overspend is caused by the two factors equally, at £100 each.

Fixed overheads variances

The fixed overheads were budgeted at £3,300, but the actual costs were only £3,000. However, with production of 200 batches, it should have taken 133.33 labour hours and the standard fixed overhead cost recovery is therefore 133.33 × £24 = £3,200. The actual cost is £100 less than the recovered cost, a favourable total fixed overhead variance.

The fixed overhead variance, like all the other variances we've seen so far, can be split into two components. The first is an overhead expenditure variance, the second the overhead volume variance.

However, the volume variance can also be further analysed into a capacity and an efficiency variance.

The *fixed overhead expenditure variance* is the difference between the budgeted overheads and the actual overheads:

= £3,300 – £3,000 = £300

The *fixed overhead capacity variance* is the difference between the actual overheads recovered (actual hours at the standard rate) and the budget overheads:

= (140 × £24) – £3,300 = £60

The *fixed overhead efficiency variance* is the standard overheads that ought to have been recovered (standard hours at the standard rate) less the actual overheads recovered:

= (133.33 × £24) – (140 × £24) = (£160).

The capacity and efficiency variances added together make up the fixed overhead volume variance.

Again, what do they actually mean?

- The efficiency variance is caused by the same as the labour and variable overhead efficiency variances – the effective use of labour for production as compared with the standard.
- The capacity variance indicates shortfalls, or otherwise, in output relative to the standard (budget), generally caused by downtime due to machine or labour availability.
- The expenditure variance simply compares how much has been spent compared with the level of expenditure that might be expected given the level of production. But since, by definition, the fixed costs bear no relation to the level of production, this is more of a mathematical variance rather than a useful management one.

Other variances

There are other variances that can be calculated to do with mix and yield, but the causes of these are often down to common sense reasons. The standards are set based on an anticipated combination of products being made and a certain quantity of each arising from a given level of input.

The variances arise when the actual mix of products is different and there is a change in the output relative to the input of raw materials. The first is usually caused by sales requiring more of one product to be made than another and the second by the efficient use of materials or otherwise.

Using variances for sales

Since variances are merely mathematical formula, they can be applied to any situation where there is a standard of performance to be compared with an actual one. This includes sales and margins.

In the same way that costs can be broken down into material, labour and overheads with price/rate and efficiency variances, so the sales results as they differ from a standard (or budget) can also be analysed. The principles are exactly the same for calculating:

- sales margin price variance
- sales margin quantity variance
- sales margin mix variance
- sales margin volume variance.

In all these, the standard sales margin is the standard selling price less the standard cost. If marginal costing is used, then the phrase 'sales margin' is simply replaced by 'sales contribution'.

Reporting variances

Like any reported information, variance analysis results should be passed on to the appropriate manager quickly. If there is too long a delay, by the time the appropriate manager has found out, it might be too late to do anything about it. In organizations practising management by exception, only those variances above a certain size are reported, avoiding time wasted reporting and acting on relatively trivial items.

The variances themselves are only indicators of potential problems and it is up to management (guided by the cost accountant to explain the origin of the figures) to determine the root causes.

Also be aware that favourable variances merit investigation too. They may indicate that the standards are too 'soft', e.g. assuming a wastage of 20% when really it is only 10% will generate a consistent favourable usage variance. It would 'hide' the fact that even 10% is being wasted and improving that would increase profitability.

Key points

- Variance analysis is the reported information on the differences between standard and actual results.
- Management by exception only brings to the attention of management those variances which are significant, whether favourable or adverse.
- The total materials variance can be further analysed into price and usage variances for each item used in a product.
- Similarly, the direct labour variance can be broken down into rate and efficiency variances.
- There are calculations for variances relating to overheads, but since overheads are not truly variable with output, these figures are not as useful to management.
- The variance methodology can also be applied to sales results.
- Variances should be reported swiftly enough to allow corrective action to be taken. Be aware that a favourable variance, when analysed, may hide an adverse one that is more than offset by a favourable one.

Investigate the cause

The calculation of variances is normally done by Accounts (although the computer helps!). Exception reporting is the most common method of passing information to management. From a top level variance (e.g. total materials variance), other variances can be calculated to show the major factors underlying the top variance. At the end of it all, management must determine precisely what activities or processes caused the variance and take suitable action. The variance is only the messenger, not the cause.

That almost wraps it up for costing, but there are a couple of interesting uses which deserve to be considered.

Chapter 12 Review Questions

1 A variance arises between which two set of figures?
2 What is the opposite of a favourable variance?
3 The sum of a materials price variance and materials usage variance make up which variance?
4 Into which elements can a direct labour variance be further analysed?
5 What is the formula to calculate a price variance?
6 What would an adverse labour efficiency variance imply about the operators?
7 Why would a favourable total materials variance of £2,000 merit further investigation?

13 two more things on costing

In this chapter you will learn
- about break even analysis
- about activity based costing
- about the limitations of abc

Break even analysis

Remember this graph from Chapter 10?

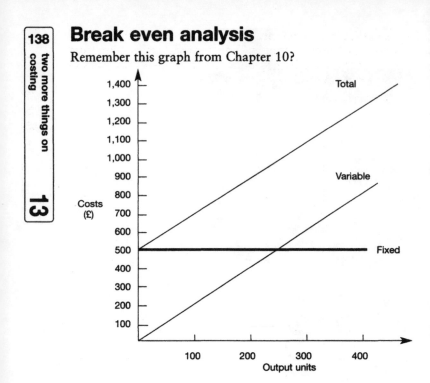

It showed the variable, fixed and total costs of car battery production, based on the following table of data:

Quantity	100	200	300	400
Variable costs (£)	200	400	600	800
Fixed costs (£)	500	500	500	500
Total costs (£)	700	900	1,100	1,300

It is a very useful graph for showing cost–volume–profit analysis, out of which comes break even analysis. This is much simpler than it sounds! If a business is to be profitable, it needs to have a sales revenue that is higher than all its costs – that's all there is to it. Just like Mr Micawber said in *David Copperfield*, 'Annual income twenty pounds, expenditure nineteen nineteen six, result happiness.'

Charles Dickens was probably using cash accounting in that instance.

To present it all in a very neat way, all that has to be added to the graph is another straight line showing sales units and revenue. So if the car battery manufacturer sells its products at £5 each we get the following graph:

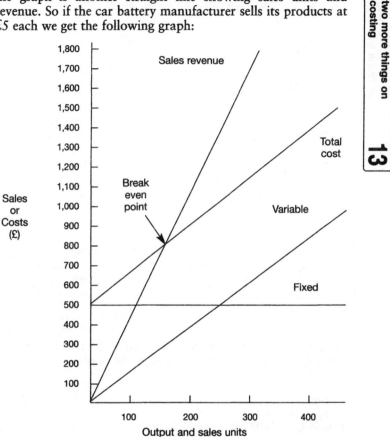

When the sales revenue line climbs above the total cost line, the company is in profit. At the precise point where the revenue equals total cost, there is the break even point. This tells management how many units have to be sold/produced to break even.

So reading from the graph, the break even point is 167 units. This can be verified with calculation:

Sales revenue 167 units @ £5 each	=	£835
Costs – variable @ £2	=	£334
– fixed	=	£500
Total	=	£834

Sales above 167 units, all else being equal, add to the profit by £3 per unit.

Because the graph is a simple diagram, it does have limitations in its use:
- A product may not have a consistent selling price; the price may have to be dropped to achieve higher volumes of sales.
- Firms usually sell more than one product, making it difficult to ascertain matching costs.
- The assumption is that fixed costs stay fixed and variable costs are truly variable in a linear fashion (the variable unit cost must always be the same).
- The graph assumes stock levels don't change or marginal costing is used, i.e. that all production is sold or costed without any overhead recovery (otherwise there would be the added complication of overheads in the stock valuation).

These points aside, break even analysis is an interesting way to start looking at profitability (or otherwise) especially for proposed products. It sets a framework for what sales are needed to achieve various levels of profit based on the costing information.

Activity based costing

Back in Chapter 10 we looked at different methods of allocating fixed overhead costs back to the products, coming up with a recovery rate.

These are all arbitrary methods, some more suitable than others depending upon the circumstances of the company (e.g. using labour hours as an allocation method is a bit silly in a capital-intensive operation where machine costs are significantly higher than labour costs).

Nor do any of the methods reduce the total costs, they just shuffle them from one place to another.

After years of thought and deliberation and a general unhappiness about the arbitrariness of the allocation methods, came a stunning piece of logic. This stated that all costs ought to be product related in some way, otherwise there would be no point in having the cost. Management consultants were needed in droves as activity based costing (ABC) was launched upon unsuspecting managers.

The broad principle is that all costs are caused by some product or other. A production planning meeting discusses products. Sales and marketing people market products. It's just a question of setting up a mechanism for recording how much time and cost is dedicated to each product and allocating the cost of the meeting or activity accordingly.

ABC approaches the situation like this: imagine a sales meeting where four hours are spent discussing the promotional activities for ten products. The cost of the meeting stems from the managers' time spent on it. From knowledge of the payroll costs of the individual managers attending the meeting (or an assumed hourly rate), the cost of the meeting can be ascertained. That cost is shared among the products discussed in proportion to the time spent discussing them.

In theory this is a fine idea, but it has a number of problems associated with it. First the time spent recording product-based activities swells bureaucracy, adding to the total cost (as do management consultants). Secondly, allocating the fixed costs in a more sensible manner may provide a more accurate cost for each product, but again it doesn't reduce the total costs of the company, merely moves them from one product to another.

Finally, there are still some awkward activities which just refuse to be product related – Accounts, Personnel, IT. It is possible to come up with ways of allocating those costs – if 50% of all invoices relate to Product A, it gets 50% of Accounts' costs. But now we're back into the realms of arbitrary allocations and general rules of thumb . . . back where we started really.

This is not to decry the merits of activity based costing. In some companies it has led to sensible reviews of overhead expenditure, by asking the question 'Why are we doing some things that do not appear to have any benefit?' It has also led to the realization that some products are more costly to make than previously thought, because they take up proportionally more management time (an overhead cost).

On the whole though, most companies have carried out a review of their overhead expenditure and then settled back into one of the more familiar ways of overhead allocation, perhaps refining

it a little in the light of their ABC experiences. They are prepared to trade simplicity for a little inaccuracy.

Key points

- **Break even analysis** – is a simple but effective comparison of revenues and costs (variable and fixed) to determine volumes required to achieve profitability.
- **Activity based costing** – was proposed on the basis that all costs are incurred for a reason which can usually be traced back to a product, that is then given those costs. This is a more equitable way of assigning costs to products than some arbitrary methods, but requires much effort to do it properly.

Who guards the guards?

The Accounts department is the bearer of financial information. We have seen the format of published accounts and now know what goes into making the numbers.

The public (including investors, competitors, suppliers, employees etc.) are entitled to rely upon the accuracy and validity of the numbers on the accounts. But who checks them and confirms that what the company declares is correct?

The auditors do.

Chapter 13 Review Questions

1 What does the break even point signify?
2 What are the restrictions on the use of break even analysis?
3 What makes activity based costing a more scientific approach to the allocation of fixed overhead costs?
4 So why hasn't it been universally adopted?

14

the audit of annual accounts

In this chapter you will learn
- why an annual audit is required
- what happens in an audit
- about auditors and the audited
- about the scope and responsibility of auditors

Who is an auditor?

Auditors are accountants too. As members of the Institute of Chartered Accountants in England and Wales (ICAEW), the Institute of Chartered Accountants in Scotland, or the Irish Institute, they are the only people allowed, by company law, to audit the accounts of limited companies.

Don't you trust me?

The accounts for a company are prepared by the accountants who are employed by it. They are usually qualified themselves, perhaps with the ICAEW or one of the other professional bodies (see Appendix A for the differences, real and perceived). So surely the accounts will be all right – there's no need to have them audited, is there?

In the vast majority of cases, there are no problems. The auditor confirms the figures prepared by the company, adds a statement to the accounts to that effect and then moves on to their next audit.

The need for an audit

There was a time when auditors weren't needed. Many years ago, most organizations were run by the people who had put up the money to start with. As commerce and trade expanded, large amounts of capital were required to put expensive machines in big buildings and businesses became too big for the owners to run by themselves. This meant that the investors were not necessarily also the managers of the company.

Now that in itself was not a problem. Except that the managers were responsible for reporting what the profits of the company were to the owners and when there was not sufficient profit made to pay a dividend to the owners, the owners wanted proof that this was the case. The owners may have become a mite suspicious, especially when the managing director started driving a new-fangled Henry Ford machine.

So an independent authority was established and company law passed, so that all companies which had limited liability to their creditors (instead of unlimited personal liability of the owners or managers – see Appendix B) had to have their annual accounts audited. This validation and verification could only be done by suitably qualified people – Chartered accountants.

An audit in practice

What actually happens in an audit is that the company's accountant prepares the figures, as agreed by the board of directors (who bear ultimate responsibility for the figures – they literally have to sign them before they are sent to Companies House). The auditors then turn up and begin to check the numbers.

Now if a company reports sales of £15,252,368, the auditors do not go through all the invoices and credit notes issued that year and add them all up to verify the total. Instead they do sample checks, picking out a few (generally high value) invoices and asking to see proofs of delivery and that the customer has paid the invoice (unless it is still showing in the debtors ledger).

The auditors issue circulation letters to the top few debtors and creditors, asking them to confirm the balances that the company is showing in its year end accounts. After all, stating in the accounts that British Airways owes the company £3,000,000 might make a significant contribution to the assets of the company – but if British Airways only agree to owing £400,000, something's wrong somewhere.

So that is the approach of the auditors – not to check that everything is right – but to see if something might be wrong. They have only a limited time in which to complete the audit, possibly as little as a week for a company with a turnover of less than £5m.

Another problem the auditors face is that they usually have very limited knowledge of the systems of the company they are checking. Different companies have different computers, different procedures, and the auditors have to fathom these out during their short time there.

Rules of engagement

Fortunately for the auditors, they are not required to get all 'i's and 't's dotted and crossed. They use a concept of materiality. So what if a credit note for £1,500 missed the cut off at the end of the financial year? If sales are £10m, then the amount of the credit note is neither here nor there. It's not significant enough to have the accounts changed – it is immaterial.

One of the rules that auditors must follow is to ensure that the accounts are *prudent* and *conservative* in their reporting of profitability. This means, if the auditor is in any doubt, the profits should be understated so as not to mislead current and prospective investors as to the merits of the organization. So they check that stock is not overvalued (by comparing prices paid for the items with their unit value in stock) and how currency exchange differences are included or otherwise in profit, amongst other things.

The auditors will also be looking for consistency in the way the figures have been prepared. Given that some of the rules for accountancy are somewhat flexible, it is important that those who want to use the company's accounts can compare like with like. So if the company depreciated plant and machinery over five years last year, it ought to do the same this year. The management cannot suddenly decide that because profits are a bit on the low side, a ten-year depreciation policy would improve the results. At least, if they did change the depreciation policy, the auditors would want a better explanation.

At the very least, if there is a change in any accounting policy, it has to be declared in a note to the accounts for the first year of change. This does reveal to the alert reader of the accounts that something is afoot.

Relationship between auditors and management

The auditors are utterly independent of the company and its management. But they are paid by the company to carry out the audit.

Some uncharitable minds might suggest that this puts the auditors in a difficult situation. After all, although the directors are obliged by law to appoint auditors to make the independent checks, there is no obligation on the company to keep the same audit firm year in and year out. So does this mean, if the auditors find something they are not happy with, they simply ignore it for fear of upsetting the directors and losing a lucrative fee? (Some audit fees for major plcs run into millions of pounds. But note that the cost of the audit is always isolated in the notes to the accounts.)

No, of course not. The upper hand is with the auditors, for two reasons.

1 If the auditors are insistent that the accounts, as they stand, are not correct, they can refuse to sign them off (approve them as being accurate) or give them only qualified approval. That tells readers of the accounts that there's something odd, but that the auditors and the management couldn't agree on who was right. At the very best, this is a disastrous piece of public relations for the company, since outsiders will wonder what is going on with the company's financial reporting.

2 The directors are entitled to appoint new auditors. However, the replacement auditors will be highly suspicious of why their predecessors were removed – it's an uncommon thing for auditors to be changed. They will be on their guard immediately for any signs of wrongdoing.

There are grey areas in accounting, such as brand valuation, where the management may feel they are right and want to stick to their guns. The auditors may simply possess a different opinion, but if it is one they are strongly convinced of, the accounts will not get full approval.

Changing the auditors

Appointing new auditors is a simple task, done at the annual general meeting. In an agenda for such a meeting, there is usually a resolution to re-appoint the current auditors for the next year, at a remuneration to be determined by the directors, or to appoint new ones.

A company can keep the same auditors for years and it is this cosy relationship which bothers some people. There is a suggestion, which may come into legal force eventually, that companies should be compelled to change their auditors every three years or less. This would prevent audit firms from being overreliant on next year's audit fee – and if they're going to lose the business anyway, they might as well be as forthright as necessary. But it could just become a game of musical auditors, with auditors swapping companies.

The stamp of approval

So, if everything has gone well, the accounts will be published and filed at Companies House for all to see. In the accounts there is a page signed by the auditors, declaring the accounts to be, in their opinion, a 'true and fair view' of the financial state of the company.

So that means – what? A true view? There is no definition in company law of what a true view is or, for that matter, a fair one. So does true mean accurate or correct? We already know that auditors operate with a level of materiality, so the numbers don't have to be spot on. It's more likely that 'true' is used to mean 'true as opposed to false'.

'Fair' is a little harder to understand. It seems to imply that the numbers probably, in the opinion of the auditors, give a pretty reasonable idea of what's gone on in the company over the last year. It's all a bit vague really.

Believing what you see

Still, if the accounts have been signed off by the auditors, surely they must be right?

Not according to the auditors.

There has been a legal case in which investors relied on the audited accounts when making their decision to put money into the company. Unfortunately, it turned out that there must have been something wrong somewhere, because they lost their money. Naturally, they blamed the auditors for producing a report that, they felt, was utter rubbish.

Not our fault you lost your money, claimed the auditors. For one thing, it now appears that the directors of the company didn't tell us everything that was going on – if they had, we wouldn't have approved the accounts. Furthermore, they suggested, you shouldn't use the accounts as a basis for investment.

This was a major denial of the auditors' responsibility – what use are published accounts if even the auditors say you can't actually rely upon them?

The claims of the auditors were understandable. If they had agreed liability, it would have set a very expensive precedent leading to claims for damages by investors who felt they had been misled by information in approved accounts.

But the courts agreed that the auditors did owe a *duty of care* to readers of the accounts and that they cannot just wash their hands of the whole thing. However, the investors' case was weakened because they ought to have taken other financial information (presumably historic records, performances of competitors and the industry) into account – the accounts of the company should have formed only a part of their knowledge before deciding to invest.

The credibility of audited accounts, and auditors in particular, took a heavy knock in this sad episode. It's a pity really, because the vast majority of accounts are probably perfectly all right, but the media aren't interested in those cases.

Key points

- An audit is compulsory for limited companies and must be done by suitably qualified practitioners.
- Auditors are independent of the company employing them.
- The auditors only have a limited time in which to complete their work, so they principally test the validity of transactions and results, rather than rigorously checking everything.
- If the auditors do not agree with the financial results as prepared by the company and the directors will not change them, the auditors can refuse to approve the accounts or give them only qualified approval.
- Legal precedent now suggests that, although the auditors have a duty of care to those who read the accounts, potential investors cannot rely entirely upon the accounts as a basis for a decision.

Next ...

Even though the accounts have to be passed by the auditors, there is still some scope for the company's accountants to interpret the rules to suit their purpose. There's nothing illegal in this – some of the accounting regulations have a certain amount of flexibility. You need to know about this flexibility so that when you are trying to interpret a set of accounts, you can tell what they mean.

Chapter 14 Review Questions

1 Why is an audit needed?

2 Who is ultimately responsible for the accuracy of the accounts?

3 How can the auditors confirm individual debtor and creditor balances?

4 What if the directors and the auditors don't agree on the contents and accuracy of the accounts? Who wins?

5 How are the auditors changed?

6 Where can you get a set of statutory accounts for any limited company?

7 How useful are the accounts in assessing the investment potential of a company?

15 tricks of the trade

In this chapter you will learn
- how companies influence how figures are reported
- what is meant by creative accounting
- how to use this knowledge when reading statutory reports

Same only different

Very few published accounts are fraudulent and designed to mislead the reader. This would be a dangerous game to play because, if incorrect information is spotted by the auditors, they will qualify their approval of the accounts, or worse still, refuse to sign them. It could have dramatic consequences for the share price and inevitably the careers of the directors.

But even so, the rules of accounting allow the directors some flexibility in how various figures are arrived at. In order to be able to understand and compare the results of different companies, you need to be aware of the variations that may be used to arrive at their respective numbers. Profit in one company is not necessarily profit as understood by another!

Common sleights of hand

There are a number of ways a company can influence the reported figures. They may choose a way of accounting for certain transactions that others may do differently. If you are going to try and compare accounts, you must allow for these differences – if you can spot them.

Capitalizing costs

Take for instance the case of a retail company that has decided to build two new and identical superstores. They each cost £10m to build.

The first is paid for in cash. A cheque for £10m goes to Mr Builder & Sons and the new building is entered in the company's accounts as a fixed asset with a gross book value based on its cost, £10m.

All companies would treat an asset purchased like this in this way, with the intention of depreciating it over, say, 25 years. The annual depreciation charge would then be £400,000.

The second building is to be financed by a loan taken out to pay Mr Builder. The interest is £100,000 a year for five years, over which time the loan is paid off in full.

Now some companies determine that the interest payable on the loan to build the superstore is, in fact, an intrinsic cost of the building. In this case, the interest is added to the £10m building cost and the accounting transaction is to enter the building as a fixed asset with an original gross book value of £10.5m (the actual cost of the building, £10m, plus the interest of £500,000).

Yet the second building is exactly the same as the first. Mr Builder received £10m in each case. It's surely common sense that one cannot be valued at more than the other? It can under accounting rules (common sense doesn't come into it).

Even so, not all companies will capitalize the interest. Interest is usually deducted from profits – capitalizing it effectively spreads that cost over the economic life of the asset and is deducted from the profits in the form of depreciation over several years.

So if there were two identical companies, one of which treated the interest as an expense and the other as a capital item, the profits of the first would be lower in the first five years as it wrote off the interest. Thereafter, its annual profit would appear higher, because the second company would have a higher depreciation charge due to the interest being written off in line with the original asset. This comparison is shown below.

Deductions from profit (£000s):

1 *Interest treated as an expense*

Year	1	2	3	4	5	6	...	25
Depreciation	400	400	400	400	400	400	...	400
Interest	100	100	100	100	100	–	...	–
Total	500	500	500	500	500	400	...	400

2 *Interest capitalized (depreciation = £10,500,000/25)*

Year	1	2	3	4	5	6	...	25
Depreciation	420	420	420	420	420	420	...	420
Total	420	420	420	420	420	420	...	420

So, in the early years after building the superstore, capitalizing the interest improves profits by £80,000 a year, not a small amount (although it may be relatively small in relation to the company's overall performance). From the sixth year onwards, the first method has now written off all the interest and has a depreciation charge £20,000 less than the other. After 25 years, they will both come out the same, having deducted £10,500,000 from profits all together. It's the timing of the deductions that is different.

Neither method is right or wrong, but it is important to notice the rules companies are using if you wish to compare their results.

The expense versus capital issue is not just for interest – it extends to R&D costs, patents, goodwill (the difference between the amount paid to acquire another company and its 'fair' value), and it's even been used for employee costs!

Revaluation of fixed assets

This has been explained before. Just be aware that, overnight, the Balance Sheet will show an increase in the company's book value, although the accounting rules are sensible enough to prevent the increase directly affecting the profit. It makes a difference to the apparent worth of the business and to the balance sheet ratios though.

Brand accounting

In the same way that fixed assets can be revalued, an extra asset for the deemed value of the company's brands can suddenly materialize. The principle is that, under normal circumstances, the Balance Sheet does not reflect the intangible assets of the company, such as the strength of its brand names. If the company has a well known brand name or image (e.g. Mars, Reebok, Xerox), where is the value of that name in the financial reports? Nowhere.

In theory, this understates the value of the company in its Balance Sheet. In practice, management consultants have earned a few bob helping companies to value their brands. Think of any major brand for any product and the reputation it has attached to it. How many millions would a new company have to spend to achieve the same level of recognition? That's the argument for a brand value appearing on a Balance Sheet. Against it is the fact that it is (a) valuing thin air and (b) entirely subjective. But it still happens, although many are not happy with it.

Depreciation policy

The theory is that individual fixed assets are depreciated over their useful economic life. In practice, assets are grouped together into categories and depreciated over a standard number of years. Vehicles are usually depreciated over four years, even though a fork lift truck may actually run for fifteen years and a distribution lorry replaced every two.

So the first thing to watch out for is the respective policies of companies being compared. Depreciating over more years gives a lower depreciation charge to the Profit and Loss Account each year, but if the asset is sold or replaced when it still has a book value, there will be a comparatively large deduction from the profit.

Bertwear Limited and Caramaway Limited each buy a new paint spraying machine costing £80,000. Their respective depreciation policies for plant and machinery are five and ten years using the straight line method. After six years, the machines are replaced by better technology and each is sold for £12,000. The effects on profit are shown below.

	Bertwear	Caramaway
Depreciation charge	(£)	(£)
Year 1	(16,000)	(8,000)
Year 2	(16,000)	(8,000)
Year 3	(16,000)	(8,000)
Year 4	(16,000)	(8,000)
Year 5	(16,000)	(8,000)
Year 6	–	(8,000)
Gain/(loss) on disposal	+12,000	(20,000)
Total	(68,000)	(68,000)

The £20,000 loss on disposal for Caramaway comes from:

Gross book value	80,000
Accumulated depreciation	(48,000)
Net book value	32,000
Proceeds from sale	12,000
Net loss	20,000

The total effect on the two companies has to be the same, after all they've done exactly the same thing. However, the timing of the reported profit is different.

Bertwear adopted a more prudent policy and wrote off the asset quicker, with reduced profits. Caramaway had a smaller reduction in its profits in those years, but made a loss on disposal of the machine because it still carried a value in its Balance Sheet. For Bertwear the machine did not have a book value on sale, having been fully written off by then, so the proceeds were pure profit. Again it's a timing difference – costs can be defrayed to later years, improving the short-term profits. It's one to watch out for.

More obvious is a change in depreciation policy by a company, if only because such a change has to be openly declared in a note to the accounts, preferably with some sort of justification.

To be helpful, many companies will state what the depreciation charge would have been under the old policy to allow you to compare. Changes are usually brought about when redefining the useful economic life of asset groups – in some industries, advancements in technology may be so fast that it is wise to depreciate assets over three years instead of five. Conversely, the company may adopt such a positive maintenance program that it feels justified in extending the depreciation lifespan of its plant and machinery from five to seven years (with a corresponding lower depreciation charge and subsequent increase in reported profit).

Keep your eyes open

By the time you can get hold of a copy of a company's accounts, several months will have passed from the date to which they refer. Bear in mind that the Balance Sheet represents only one day in the activities of the company. The day after, anything could have happened.

In fact, it is common practice for companies to restrict payments to suppliers as the financial year end approaches. This makes the cash figure in the accounts look better (and the creditors higher). Invariably, in the few days following the year end, the money goes flooding out to pacify the patient creditors, but that doesn't get reported anywhere.

So don't rely entirely on the accounts to understand a company. Read them, interpret them, and get further information from other sources – financial press, local media, customers, competitors, the company itself, employees. They will know more about the current affairs than the accounts can ever tell you. The numbers are just part of the information available, albeit a very good part.

Key points

- The rules and regulations of financial reporting are not always black or white – shades of grey allow creative and artistic interpretation in preparing the financial results. Be aware of whether you are comparing like with like.
- Never take the stated profit for granted, check what accounting policies and assumptions have been used to determine the profit figure.
- Accounting information is historical and soon becomes out of date, so don't use the accounts to the exclusion of all else.

Better information

Because the published accounts are available to all those who are interested, they lack detail. Certainly, the managers of the company will want more frequent and more specific information on the company's performance and they get it in the form of the management accounts.

Chapter 15 Review Questions

1 How would capitalizing the interest costs on the money borrowed to finance a new building affect

   a profits?

   b the Balance Sheet?

2 What is brand accounting? Why is it controversial?

16

financial information for managers

In this chapter you will le...
- how to use financial information
- about financial and management accounting
- about management accounting, ratios and decision making

Saving up for rainy days

It could be said that there are more than one set of financial results for a company. The first is the one the accountant prepares to establish the numbers she's happy with. This can be adjusted to allow for any discrepancies that may come to light later on, just in case something has been missed. The accountant has a bit up her sleeve, so to speak.

The accountant's version forms the results given to the managing director. He may think that the results are awfully good this month, so why doesn't the accountant squirrel some of it away in case next month isn't so good? A couple more simple journals could provide for some potential costs to reduce the profits nicely.

When it comes to the financial year end, all those bits up sleeves or squirrelled away either have to be put back into the accounts or explained to the auditors (assuming the auditors find them). This will be the basis of the 'real' results but, for various reasons, management may want to move the profit up or down. They might do a little extra writing off of stock, fixed assets or bad debtors, or try to have stock revalued a little higher. Generally it is easier to lose some of the profit than add to it. Some of the reasons for adjusting the declared profit include:
- preferring to show steady, rather than exceptional, growth against last year, because the shareholders might expect the same again next year; it's much easier to maintain a pattern of 3% growth each year and it looks better than reporting, for example, +8%, +1%, −1%, +4% in consecutive years
- taxable losses brought forward
- knowing that customers and competitors will see the results (would you be happy if a supplier was making very large profits?).

Financial v. management accounts

As we saw earlier, the financial accounts are those published, filed at Companies House and available for anyone to examine. They contain the Profit and Loss Account, a Balance Sheet and a Cash Flow Statement, with some explanatory notes for some of the figures.

They also leave many questions unanswered.

The management accounts, on the other hand, have a restricted circulation because they are much more detailed. The management accounts are usually more than just a set of accounts – it is frequently a whole pack of financial information, often accompanied by non-financial data such as head counts, production quantities and commentaries from various managers explaining what has happened in the period and why.

This pack tends to be very focused on the profit and loss side of operations, rather than the Balance Sheet. This is because:

1 most non-financial managers feel they understand sales and costs better than things like debtors, creditors, lease obligations and other Balance Sheet items
2 those same managers feel that sales and costs are under their control, whilst those Balance Sheet lines are the responsibility of the Accounts department.

The first point can be overcome by education (such as reading a good book on the subject!).

The second point is understandable when you consider that the Accounts department is responsible for collecting money and paying it out. However, when enlightenment comes, these managers will realize that the sources of debtors and creditors are sales and purchases respectively, and these are not Accounts functions! The level of creditors to be paid depends upon the purchases made and most managers make purchases of one sort or another. The fewer purchases made, the less stock and creditors there are, with less demand on cash to pay them.

Contents of the management accounts pack

The key document is the Profit and Loss Account, or it may be referred to as an Income or Operating Statement. Like the P&L Account in the financial accounts, it will start with sales, although there may be some simple analysis such as home/export or own sales/factored. (Factored sales are those made when finished goods from another company are sold straight on without changing them, so the company is in effect a distributor. The distinction is not always important, except sales of own-produced items tend to be more profitable.)

Then comes the cost of sales, deducted from sales to give a gross margin.

Overheads in management accounts are usually reported at departmental level, whereas they can be summarized in financial accounts. Department heads are responsible for the expenditure within their departments and so need to know what the actual results are, preferably against budget.

Deducting overheads from gross margin produces an operating profit. Depreciation may be charged as a single figure or allocated to departments (in line with their use of fixed assets), depending upon the company's (or accountant's) philosophy.

Often this is as 'low' as management accounts go. Although the financial accounts have more lines, with deductions for interest and tax, management accounts are for the use of managers in their daily operational activities. Interest and taxation rates are generally beyond their control, although hopefully not their understanding.

The rest of the pack

In no particular order, the rest of the management accounts may include the following financial information.

Sales and margin analysis

This breaks down the sales and margin for the month, usually by customer, as shown below.

	£
Norrison	212,020
B&B	70,412
Ohio Stores	44,885
Spanners	22,694
Doricos	18,936
Tristram	15,220
Other	40,650
Total	424,817

The analysis could be by customer category or type (DIY centre, superstore, etc.) if that would be more useful to management, or even by product (individual, range or group).

Alongside the sales figure, the gross margin can also be shown – if it is known of course (it could be derived from the costing system, actual or standard). It is certainly a useful thing to be aware of – compare this table with the previous one which had sales only:

	Sales (£)	Margin (£)	%
Norrison	212,020	50,650	23.8
B&B	70,412	24,298	34.5
Ohio Stores	44,885	21,640	48.2
Spanners	22,694	11,395	50.2
Doricos	18,936	7,222	38.1
Tristram	15,220	2,350	15.4
Other	40,650	14,612	35.9
Total	424,817	132,167	31.2

Suddenly doing business with Norrison doesn't seem that great. Perhaps more emphasis should be placed on increasing sales to Ohio and Spanners, and maybe Tristram should be dropped altogether – after taking into consideration selling and distribution costs, this business may run at a loss.

Before jumping to such conclusions though, more information is needed. This is only one month's results and it may not be a fair reflection of the normal sales and margin. Adding a year to date column would be useful.

Also, the margin obviously depends on the products sold to each of the customers. If Norrison buys something made uniquely for them, which other customers don't want, then high sales at a lower margin may be acceptable. However, the questions raised are perfectly valid and more information should lead to informed decisions about doing business with each of the customers.

Customer and product profitability

Following the same process as the sales and margin analysis, the profitability of each customer or product can be determined theoretically.

In practice, this involves allocating the more obviously relevant costs, like selling and distribution, to each customer or product. If a sales rep is dedicated to two accounts and he spends his time equally on each, allocate half of his cost to each customer.

Transport costs are probably allocated on the share of sales total each customer has, which is as good an arbitrary way as any.

Generally, such a profitability analysis will stop there. Allocating further costs becomes a guessing game (unless the company is using Activity Based Costing). For example, carving up the administration costs between customers is likely to be done on some estimated basis and may cloud the issue. What the managers are really looking for is an indication of which customers and products are making the most significant contributions to the company's profitability. Armed with that information, they can decide how to proceed with each customer or product – whether to develop it, drop it or just leave it alone.

Overheads statements

From the Profit and Loss Account in the management accounts pack, a departmental manager can see how his total spend relates to his budget – is he over or under?

But knowing that he is over or under is not enough – he needs to know in what areas the variance occurred.

An overheads statement for each department will provide that information. It is a list of the expenditure by type of cost, invariably from the classification used in the general ledger.

Overhead statement July 2006 – R&D department

	Month			Year to date		
	Actual	Budget	Var	Actual	Budget	Var
	(£)	(£)	(£)	(£)	(£)	(£)
Salaries	1,200	1,400	200	3,900	4,400	500
NIC	122	145	23	396	448	52
Pension	90	95	5	280	300	20
Stationery	250	100	(150)	400	320	(80)
Plant hire	120	80	(40)	600	250	(350)
Patents	2,500	1,000	(1,500)	4,000	3,000	(1,000)
Consultancy	400	0	(400)	900	0	(900)
Depreciation	450	450	0	2,000	2,000	0
Total	5,132	3,270	(1,862)	12,476	10,718	(1,758)

This is a common format for an overhead expenditure statement, showing actual costs against budget with the difference (variance), for the period and the financial year to date.

Overall, the R&D manager has overspent by nearly £1,800 against the budget in the year to date, but the detail contains some interesting points.

The costs relating to salaries are all lower than budget – is the department understaffed? Has this led to the need to use consultants, the cost of which were not budgeted?

The patents cost highlights a common problem with comparing actuals and budgets – phasing. Usually budgets for overhead expenditures are set in total for the year – in this case patents £12,000 – and then phased into accounting periods, often just dividing by the number of periods. It can be done more accurately – electricity and gas costs tend to be higher in winter than summer – but for the sake of ease and convenience, it's often done by dividing the total for the year into equal shares.

Yet the nature of patent fees means making occasional lump sum payments, whereas the budget is spread equally over the year. The current variance might be due to a timing issue and, no doubt, the R&D manager will defend the overspend by saying that the total will be back in line with budget by the year end. He may argue that he only needs one 'free' month, with no actual spend against a budget of £1,000, to be back in line.

Depreciation is for the fixed assets that the department use – perhaps several PCs and various electrical and mechanical devices which are as mysterious to accountants as ledgers are to engineers. If the depreciation is over budget, the manager might feel aggrieved – after all, he doesn't directly control the depreciation charge, although it is related to the cost of the fixed assets that the department acquires.

It should be confirmed that the costs on the overhead statement are based on accruals *and* invoices, not just invoices. So as long as the Accounts department is aware that the R&D boffins hired a milling machine in September, but the supplier hasn't invoiced for it yet, an accrual is made to put the cost in the correct accounting period.

Ratios for management

Just as there are ratios for use by those wishing to analyse the financial accounts of a company so they can compare its performance with last year or with competitors, so there are ratios which can be used by the management. These usually compare figures with the budget or last year's performance – a stock turnover ratio of 4 may be good, bad or indifferent, but we can't tell unless there is a point of comparison.

Some of the ratios are the same as those used in analysing the financial accounts:
- stock turnover
- debtors days
- creditor days.

Others can only be determined with knowledge of what is in the more detailed management accounts, rather than the summarized information shown in the published financial accounts.

Percentage margin by customer/product – although discussed previously, this ratio is repeated here for emphasis. The financial accounts give no details of sales by individual customer and knowing where the margin is being made can help managers determine where the focus of effort ought to be.

Sales per employee – this ratio can be worked out from the published accounts, since one of the notes to the accounts is the average number of employees during the year. However, management can have this information on a monthly basis. It is more important in some industries than others, especially if the company has the ability to hire and fire temporary and casual workers.

Industry based ratios – such as sales per square foot for retail stores. Unobtainable from the financial accounts, these ratios serve as comparison of efficient use of assets (floor space) between stores of the company and industry averages (often available from marketing data companies).

Added value – a statement of added value may appear in the published accounts. It is certainly often a key feature of the glossy brochures produced by plcs. Added value represents the wealth created by the company in turning purchased items into sold ones. Mathematically, it is sales less the cost of bought in goods and services.

The difference between added value and profit is all the other expenses – wages or salaries, interest, tax and dividends.

Added value can be used, alongside profit, as a measure of the company's ability to make a whole worth more than the sum of its parts – for example, a Jaguar is worth more than the individual elements of its engine, chassis, body, interior etc.

Other information for managers

There is other financial information available which may be included in the management accounts pack, or reported separately, perhaps even on an ad hoc basis when required.

Slow moving and obsolete stock items – most stock control systems can produce a list of items which have few or no sales over a long period. The list will give quantity and value, and it encourages management to do one of two things – make a special effort to sell these products, perhaps at a lower than normal price, or to write them off (scrap them from the stock records and take the loss). Selling them at below cost will minimize the amount of the loss and at least generate some cash.

Overdue debtors listing – this may be combined with a sales versus credit limit report by customer, but in its pure form, shows which customers are currently late in settling their accounts. What action is taken depends upon the status of the debt, the customer, the company and the management attitude. The result can be anything from doing nothing, to putting a stop on any further sales to the company, to initiating legal action to recover the debt.

There is also a stop list, indicating which customers should not have any more orders accepted. Customer accounts may be put on stop for being overdue with payment (usually considerably overdue or for a significant amount) or because the customer has gone over the credit limit that the Sales and Accounts departments feel happy with. Who goes on stop is usually a matter of discussion between Accounts and Sales – often a matter of disagreement and contention!

Purchases by supplier – by knowing how much has been spent with any given supplier, a buyer may be in a strong position to negotiate for reduced prices. It is surprising how few companies track this, even though they monitor their sales to individual customers.

If expenditure is big enough, the buyer may even seek to get a retrospective rebate on the grounds of the value of the account.

A note of caution

It is common for divisions within a company (or companies within a group) to be measured by their profitability. Depending upon the nature of the business, it may be that one division is a major supplier to another in the group. Therefore, its profitability (and that of the other division) is influenced by how much it charges for the goods and services provided. The price of doing so is known as the transfer price.

Division A makes 50,000 gear boxes a year, selling 30,000 to Division B which puts them in industrial machine engines. What should be the selling price of the gear boxes to Division B, given the following information?

Cost of manufacture (Division A)	£110
List selling price (to third parties)	£300
Average selling price (after discounts, etc.)	£260

Given that the management of each division is going to be judged on its profitability, the managers of Division A will try to justify a price of £300. After all, that's what they quote to all customers to start with.

Division B's management will argue that the two divisions should be viewed as parts of a whole; that Division A is simply a manufacturing process within the group and that it is nonsense to suggest that any profit arises until the completed product (i.e. their engine) is sold to a third party. So the transfer price should be the cost price of £110. Of course, this means that Division A will make no profit on gear boxes sold to Division B, but that's not B's problem.

Usually the matter is decided by head office, which often chooses an 'arm's length transaction' philosophy – the divisions deal with each other as if they had no corporate connection. That may lead to the average selling price of £260. But what if B could buy from another supplier at £245? That would lower its costs and improve its profits. Division A would lose sales, and that £245 per gear box would be going to a company outside the group instead of keeping it all in-house. So should Division A have to lower its price to match?

This would lead to sub-optimization; instead of the profit element of gear boxes remaining within the company (either division), it is given to the outside supplier. That would be as daft as a railway company using road haulage to transport the diesel required for its engines!

This can be a very important decision, not only for its impact on local management. Consider that the two divisions are in different countries: Division A's country has a corporation tax rate of 40%; it is only 15% in Division B's country. It makes financial sense to have as much of the profit in Division B, so a low transfer price is used, perhaps even below cost. (The tax authorities of individual countries try to keep an eye out for such transactions.)

Non-financial information

Of course, there is nothing to prevent non-financial information being included when the management accounts pack is circulated. Sales and production data often appear, with comments from the responsible managers as to what has happened and why, hopefully informing other managers which issues should be addressed next.

Key points

- There may be 'hidden' sets of accounts, depending upon what results may be desirable or acceptable. However, in practice, it is difficult to make these vary too wildly from the real results.
- Management accounts are more useful than financial accounts and are not as easy to get hold of. The management accounts pack will contain some good analysis of the basic Profit and Loss Account figures, which also lend themselves to ratio analysis.
- Non-financial information may also be included.
- Transfer pricing determines the price of goods sold between two divisions in the same company, or two companies in the same group. It can be set at the market price, decided by head office, or worked out another way. The price will determine which of the divisions will make how much of the profit and so internal pricing can be a sensitive decision.

Learning new tricks

By now you are pretty knowledgeable about what accountants get up to and are ready to start playing them at their own game.

When trying to get major capital expenditure plans approved, financial justification is the key to success. Instead of letting the accountants run through your project, next we will cover what you need to do to get that approval.

Chapter 16 Review Questions

1 Which financial statements form the contents of the financial accounts?

2 What reports might be the typical contents of a management accounts pack?

3 What is an overheads statement?

4 What problems arise when one division in a company sells to another?

17

capital investment appraisal: experts only!

In this chapter you will lea[rn]
- how capital investment i[s]
  managed
- how capital expenditure [is]
  managed
- how to establish financia[l]
  project viability
- about discounted cash f[low]
  techniques and project
  viability

Techniques to frighten managers

Accounting, like most professions, comes with its own jargon that its advocates like to use to impress and befuddle the outside world. Here are some common and perfectly valid accounting methods used in evaluating capital projects, explained in everyday language.

Capital investment appraisal

Many managers are given a certain amount of discretion over the amounts of money they are permitted to spend without referring to a higher level of authority. Even when the items are of a capital nature (which is essentially a fixed asset), they can still go ahead on their own judgement up to a specified amount.

Beyond the prescribed limits, such expenditure is passed to higher levels for approval, the ultimate authority being the board of directors. If the sum of money requested is large enough, they will want to see some financial justification for the expenditure.

Although this usually applies to capital expenditure (new machinery, building extension etc.), approval can also be required for other projects which need considerable amounts of cash. Marketing projects for new product launches and R&D projects for new products and processes are good candidates for the appraisal techniques about to be discussed.

Above all, the techniques attempt to demonstrate whether the proposed project is justified financially. You might think that all the directors would want to know is 'Does the project make a profit?', but these techniques go beyond that. They are principally concerned with the cash flows of the project, not its accounting profit. By now you should appreciate the distinction.

Capital expenditure – the administration

Where there's money involved, Accounts usually have a form for it. The form will have different names in different companies, but a typical Capital Expenditure Request from will contain all or some of the details on this example:

Capital expenditure request

Date: 30 Jun 2006   **Capex No.**: 47/06

Description: 30' conveyor belt with spare motor and baling accessories

Timing of expenditure: 02/06 **(MM/YY)**

Asset category: P&M   **Lease or Buy**: Buy

Preferred supplier: Conveyors-R-Us

Alternative quotes attached: No

Initial outlay: £6,450   **Payment terms**: 60 days

Reason: C   (C = Cost saving   R = Revenue increase
                            X = R&D   H = Health & Safety
                            L = Legal   O = Other)

If replacement, details of asset to be replaced:

Asset ref no: **Original cost:**

Depreciation: **Net book value:**

Proceeds: **Gain/(loss):**

Financial justification (enclose analysis):

Payback period: 2.4 years

NPV @ 10%: £2,855   **IRR:** 25.2%

Submitted by:

Approved by:

Board approval:

The *capex number* indicates this is the 47th application in the year 2006 and it is the reference number for this request.

The usual asset categories are:
- P&M – plant and machinery
- L&B – land and buildings
- F&F – fixtures and fittings
- OE – office equipment
- Veh – cars and vehicle.

The category will indicate to Accounts the length of time over which the asset will be depreciated.

If the new asset replaces an existing one, the old one needs to be eliminated from the accounts.

The financial justification analysis is the crucial part for getting a request accepted.

Payback method

This is the simplest way of looking at the financial viability of a project. All it asks is 'How long will it be before the money needed to finance the project is recovered from the income generated by the project?'

The Production Director of Caliban Ltd proposes to the board a project for two robotic assembly machines, each costing £125,000 to buy. Running costs are £20,000 p.a. for each machine, but when fully functioning after a year, they will replace 20 employees costing £12,000 p.a. each, all of whom can be redeployed usefully elsewhere in the company (i.e. there are no redundancy costs, just a labour saving).

The payback period is calculated:

	Expenditure (£)	Savings (£)	Net (£)
Year 1	(250,000)	–	(250,000)
Year 2	(40,000)	240,000	200,000
Year 3	(40,000)	240,000	200,000

Assuming that the expenditure is phased evenly during the year, the net cash is zero after 2 years 3 months. That is the payback period of the project.

This method does suffer from some grand assumptions and over simplifications. No savings are shown in year 1 as the machines are installed and commissioned, and the labour is needed until the machines become available. According to the method, this happens precisely on day 1 of year 2 and, at the same time, the employees go to another department!

There is also the working assumption that these are cash flows, not just expenditure. Actually, cash is a more useful way of measuring results than profits – profit without a positive cash flow is potentially disastrous. If payment for the machines was delayed by a year (perhaps credit terms could be arranged so that payment need not be made until the machines are fully operational), it would reduce the payback period significantly. The method also assumes no change in stock levels, which would have to be funded if the company decided to do a little stock piling just in case something went wrong.

That said, it is a good and simple way of looking at how long it is before the company recoups its outlay and the project starts to return cash to the company. The benchmark for approval in companies using the payback method is likely to be three years or less.

However, there are more sophisticated (meaning complicated) techniques available.

Discounted cash flow – net present value

The principle behind the discounted cash flow technique is that you would rather have £1,000 today than wait a year to receive the same amount. Economists can explain it in relation to preference curves and immediate rather than delayed gratification, but the common sense view is that if you had the £1,000 now, at the very least, you could stuff it into a building society account and earn some interest on it.

In fact, that is just about the thinking behind this method of capital appraisal. The company pays interest on borrowings or forgoes interest if it has to use its own cash resources to fund projects. Hence there is a discount rate applied to cash flows, which most companies equate to the cost of money at the prevailing interest rate. To make things even easier, most companies assume a notional rate of say 8% p.a. and are happy to assess projects on that basis.

So how does it work? Consider the cash flows for a marketing campaign for the launch of a new product, Quark washing powder. Although this is not a capital expenditure project, the same principles of evaluation apply. It has an initial cash outlay with subsequent cash returns. In this example, there are also additional cash outflows required.

	Launch costs (£)	Advertising costs (£)	Sales revenues (£)	Production costs (£)
Year 1	(75,000)	(30,000)	50,000	(25,000)
Year 2	–	(30,000)	180,000	(90,000)
Year 3	–	(30,000)	160,000	(80,000)
Year 4	–	(15,000)	90,000	(45,000)
Year 5	–	(10,000)	50,000	(20,000)

The net cash flows in each year are:

	(£)
Year 1	(120,000)
Year 2	60,000
Year 3	50,000
Year 4	30,000
Year 5	20,000
Total	+40,000

A winning project? The company will be better off by £40,000 after five years. (Projects are generally cut off after five years – sometimes seven or ten – because, after that time, the figures may be nothing more than guesswork. Even before that time, they may still be quite subjective, best estimates perhaps. After all, the future cannot be predicted that accurately.)

Yet the eager accountant will want to consider the discounted cash flows. There is a horrible looking formula to describe this:

$$\text{discount factor} = \frac{1}{(1 + r)^i}$$

where r is the discount rate and i is the year number.

In English, it means that the discount factor is applied for every year that goes by. It also means that the higher the discount rate (taken as the interest rate), the less the money will be worth over the same period of time. Think of it as a sort of inflationary adjustment, when the same amount of money has less purchasing power over time.

The discount factors for 4%, 8%, 10% and 15% are as follows:

	4%	8%	10%	15%
Year 1	0.962	0.926	0.909	0.870
Year 2	0.925	0.857	0.826	0.756
Year 3	0.889	0.794	0.751	0.658
Year 4	0.855	0.735	0.683	0.572
Year 5	0.822	0.681	0.621	0.497

Using a discount rate of 15%, the value of money is halved in five years. At 4%, it takes seventeen years.

To get the discounted cash flow for any given year, multiply the cash flow in that year by the discount factor for the year, e.g. £1,000 discounted at 10% is worth £683 after four years.

Using 8%, the marketing launch project is re-evaluated:

	Net cash flow (£)	Discount rate (%)	Discounted cash flow (£)
Year 1	(120,000)	0.926	(111,120)
Year 2	60,000	0.857	51,420
Year 3	50,000	0.794	39,700
Year 4	30,000	0.735	22,050
Year 5	20,000	0.681	13,620
Total	40,000		15,670

So now the company derives only a net benefit of £15,670 when the discount factor is taken into consideration. This figure, the sum of all the discounted cash flows is called the *net present value* (NPV) of the project. It is possible for seemingly positive cash flow projects to have a negative net present value, if the major inflows of cash are later on in the life of the project and the low discount factor devalues their significance.

The NPV can also be interpreted as meaning that the company would be indifferent about going ahead with the project or receiving £15,670 now. It would accept £20,000 (or anything more than £15,670) now from a competitor not to launch the product!

The general rule is that a company will be in favour of projects that have a positive NPV and against those that are negative. This does not necessarily mean that projects with a positive NPV will be approved automatically however. It just gives them a better chance.

Discounted cash flow – internal rate of return

The corollary of the NPV method of evaluating a project is the internal rate of return (IRR) method. Instead of adding up the discounted cash flows to see whether they are positive or not, the IRR method sets out to find what discount rate would make the net present value of the project zero.

This is mathematically harder to do for the average person (including the average accountant), so it is normally done on a computer. Indeed any spreadsheet package is likely to have a specific function for working out both the NPV and the IRR for a given range of cash flows. This saves the user from having to work out and enter the formula to calculate them!

Alternatively, if you insist on having a go, guess the discount rate and work out the NPV with that rate. If the NPV is positive, try again with a higher rate – for a negative NPV, use a lower rate. Eventually, after enough goes, you will be close enough.

The IRR is given as a percentage (e.g. 'a discount rate 18.6% for this project would give an NPV of zero'). The criteria for approval of projects varies between companies, but should always exceed the cost of financing a project, usually at the prevailing interest rate. However, companies like to err on the side of caution and the pass mark, often referred to as the hurdle rate, can sometimes be around 30%.

Lease or buy

Not only can the project be valued in this way, but its method of financing can be assessed too. The cash flows of buying and leasing a capital item can be discounted and compared to find the most favourable method financially. Of course there are other considerations taken into account (such as does the company have the necessary cash to hand?).

Ranking of competing projects

If the company had an infinite amount of money then it could proceed with all those projects that have a positive NPV or whose IRR exceeds the hurdle rate. But resources are limited. There may even be projects which are mutually exclusive because of other criteria (use of a certain production line for instance). So the projects have to be given priority of preference to receive funding.

The simplest way is to declare that those with the highest NPV or IRR are those that get accepted first. However, there are other considerations that should be taken into account:

- **Absolute requirement for cash** – if a company has £2m to allocate to projects and the five candidates in order of NPV (highest first) require funding of £1.5m, £0.8m, £0.6m, £0.5m and £0.3m, it may be more beneficial to accept a combination of the lower-rated projects. If the first one is accepted at a cost of £1.5m, the next three are automatically disqualified due to insufficient funds. Alternatively, three of the other projects could be selected without exceeding the total funds available.
- **Risk** – similarly, would the company want to back just the one project? If that should turn out not to meet expectations, there is nothing else in the pipeline to recover any costs. The risk, the potential down side of each project, should be assessed before any commitment is made. Project 'Satellite launch' may have the best returns but, if it only has a 50/50 chance of succeeding, project 'Chinese kite' with half the return and a 95% chance of success may be preferable.
- **Opportunity costs** – this is a way of looking at what the company could have done instead of backing a certain project. What opportunities and rewards would it miss out on if it chose a particular project?

  Suppose a proposal to use the last 4,000 square feet of factory space for a new production line has an NPV of £33,200 over five years for an initial investment of £194,000. Accepting this precludes an offer from an outside firm which wants to rent that space for storage at £5,000 per year. The opportunity cost of increasing production facilities is £5,000 per year and should be taken into consideration.

What are the cash flows?

The following inflows and outflows are normally included in the cash flow calculation.

Inflows:
- revenues from the project (sales or cost savings)
- grants or subsidies obtained
- proceeds from the sale of fixed assets at the end of the project
- any other cash receipts as a result of the project.

Outflows:
- initial investment
- the costs of the project (materials, labour, overheads)
- working capital adjustments (increases in stocks and debtors or payments to suppliers) different to the norm
- taxation
- any other cash expenditure as a result of the project.

Be careful

Even discounted cash flow techniques have limitations. If the cash flow pattern is unusual and has an outflow after year 1, it may not be mathematically possible to calculate an IRR, or there may even be more than one! The NPV method will still work in these circumstances.

Key points
- Accounting techniques to evaluate investment proposals can be applied to any project requiring substantial funding. It also examines the best funding method – lease or buy.
- These techniques are based on the inflows and outflows of cash rather than profitability.
- The payback method looks for the cumulative cash flow to become positive within three years.
- The two discounted cash flow methods recognize the decreasing value of money over time. The net present value technique checks whether the project still has a positive return after the discount factor has been applied. The internal rate of return is the discount factor needed to make the project borderline.
- Other considerations include the ranking of projects, cash availability, risk and opportunity costs.

What else do Accounts do?

From standard financial reporting to the clever mathematics just described, accountants cover a wide range of activities. But what are the daily functions that keep the flow of financial information and analysis running along smoothly?

Chapter 17 Review Questions

1 What would a payback period of three years imply about a project?

2 What is the principle behind the discounted cash flow technique?

3 What does the net present value of a project mean?

4 How can a profitable project have a negative net present value?

5 What is the term for the discount rate that equates a project's net present value to zero?

6 For what reasons could a project with a net present value of £40,000 be preferred over one with a net present value of £60,000?

7 What activities would make up the cash flows, in and out, for a project?

18

activities of an accounts department

In this chapter you will learn
- what accounts departments do
- about sales and purchase ledgers
- about payroll and other functions
- about the general ledger
- about accounts, cash flow and financial information

What do Accounts do?

Different companies undoubtedly organize their Accounts departments in different ways, with some functions being the responsibility of other departments (sales invoicing and credit control might be under Sales; computers might be a separate department). However, by and large, the range of activities and responsibilities discussed in this chapter fall under the domain of Finance.

Sales ledger

Also known as *accounts receivable*, this function can incorporate up to three main areas:

Sales invoicing

This prepares the sales invoices (based on despatch or delivery notes) to customers. These may be typed out from the delivery note details, or automatically issued by the computer system. Responsibilities would also include raising credit notes, having first verified the customer's claim for a credit (due to short delivery, rejected items or pricing error). Note that an invoice must contain a VAT registration number (if the business is VAT registered) and a date. It also usually indicates credit terms or the due date for payment. A credit note looks very similar, except of course, it says credit note instead of invoice.

Sales ledger

This enters monies received (by cash, cheque or BACS direct into the bank) from customers, against their invoices reducing the amount owed. Payments from customers are usually accompanied by remittance advices (see below) which state the invoices that have been paid.

Theodore Enterprises Limited		
Remittance advice		
Date of payment: 28/02/06		
Invoice No	**Date of invoice**	**£**
12545	12/01/96	4,212.00
12852	28/01/96	2,515.50
Total		6,727.50

The cheque for the payment may be printed as part of the remittance or separately. Alternatively, a simple piece of paper or a compliments slip bearing the same details as above will be sufficient to let the supplier know which invoices have been paid.

To assist customers, statements (see below) are often sent out to them each month, detailing the invoices still outstanding. Indeed, some companies insist on paying 'on statement' rather than 'on invoice', which means that they will pay out once a month after they have received a statement.

Sunburst Formations Ltd
Statement of account

Customer: Stonesthrow Enterprises
Date: 31 March 2006

		Age of debt (days)		
Invoice	*Date*	*0–30*	*31–60*	*60+*
6052	16.12.05			£512.35
7145	12.01.06			£440.25
7190	17.01.06			£244.16
8333	27.02.06		£812.66	
8739	03.03.06	£416.55		
8892	06.03.06	£446.32		
Total		£862.87	£812.66	£1,196.76

Some statements just list outstanding invoices; others, like the one above, 'age' them into columns. If remittances and statements cross in the post, the statement will be out of date and incorrect.

Credit control

This involves establishing credit limits for customers (through bank and trade references) and chasing customers for payment. The latter usually starts with a telephone call, then perhaps a polite letter and eventually court proceedings if the customer continues to avoid paying. In the meantime, Credit Control should have put the customer 'on stop' (refusing to accept further orders or deliver any orders in progress) to avoid any potential loss being increased by further sales.

The setting of credit limits is based on the risk of losing sales against the risk of the customer not paying. Information used to establish the limit includes past trading experience, bank references, trade references (from other suppliers to the customer) and instinct. It can, of course, also include an analysis of the customer's accounts!

The setting of credit limits for customers and the decision to put them on stop (often a good way of encouraging customers to pay) are normally both done in consultation with the Sales department.

There is often a conflict between Credit Control which wants to stop further supplies being sent to a customer due to non-payment and the Sales department which doesn't wish to lose an account. Resolution of the conflict often comes down to judgement, but the key maxim in this situation is that a sale isn't a sale until the money comes in. Actually, in strict accounting terms, it is a sale as soon as the invoice is raised, but from a money management view, anyone can sell to someone who isn't going to pay and it doesn't matter what price you got!

So, the basic tools for cash collecting are, firstly, a telephone and, secondly, information on outstanding debts. This information comes from the sales ledger, which lists for each customer the invoices and amounts outstanding, with due dates for payment. In essence it looks like a list of statements of account for each customer.

Purchase ledger

Also called accounts payable this is the opposite side of the coin to sales ledger – dealing with suppliers. Suppliers' invoices are posted to the purchase ledger, after matching to a purchase order or delivery note, if such a system is used by the organization. If not, some other method of authorization is required, perhaps the signature of a sufficiently high-ranking manager.

Suppliers also send statements which can be reconciled to their ledger accounts. (If you think about it, your company is a customer to your suppliers.)

The purchase ledger is also the source of cheques, which are run periodically to pay suppliers. The usual routine is for the computer (or manager) to select all those invoices due to be paid by a certain date. The financial accountant, or whoever is responsible for determining how much is to be paid out overall,

has the option to edit the list, usually deleting certain suppliers from it for a number of possible reasons:
- the invoices may be in dispute (e.g. due to poor quality of product);
- there may be limited funds available to pay out;
- the supplier may also be a customer with overdue debts.

When suppliers are chasing to be paid, Accounts will check that the sum claimed agrees with what is on the purchase ledger for that supplier. The supplier's statement of account can be used for this purpose.

Payroll

The level to which payroll is carried out by an organization varies from company to company. Some will even contract out the whole job to a bureau.

Otherwise, the process can be taken from gross pay through to net pay and the paying of employees, or stop at any stage in between before it is handed over to an outside agency.

Gross pay is the total amount earned by an employee and is either hours worked times hourly rate or, for salaried employees, a fixed amount per month. On top of this, there can be numerous additions – overtime, first aid allowances, shift adjustments.

Of course, the total gross pay is not the amount the employee receives. Standard deductions are income tax (PAYE) and national insurance contributions. Further deductions are in the form of pension contributions, charitable donations, union dues and others.

All of which leaves a payslip looking like this:

Name A Zahar **NIC no.** TT 45 25 37 A **Tax code** 350L	**Payroll no.** 545 **Tax Period** 6	
	This period	Year to date
Basic pay	£1,000.00	
Overtime	£154.50	
Total Gross	£1,154.50	£7,422.65
Pension	£50.00	£300.00
Tax paid	£236.25	£1,280.00
NIC	£103.91	£668.04
Net Pay	£764.34	

Extra costs to the company are the employer's national insurance contributions (NIC), based on the employee's gross pay, and any pension contributions made by the company.

All these figures need to be worked out – the source of data is a clock card for those paid by the hour. It is much easier if the rest is done by appropriate computer programs, although there are tables available to calculate manually the correct tax and national insurance amounts, depending upon the employee's gross pay. The first chapter on personal finance (Chapter 21) goes into more detail.

Paying employees can be done by cash, bank giro transfer, BACS or, less commonly, by cheque. Giro transfer and BACS make the payment directly into an employee's bank account, while cash payments can be made by an outside firm for added security. Employees are given payslips to notify them of their earnings and deductions.

The payroll department works out the amounts to be paid to the DSS/Inland Revenue for the NIC and tax deducted, plus the employer's NIC. This is paid monthly. Pension contributions are handed over to the pension fund managers (usually an insurance firm) according to stipulated frequencies, again usually monthly.

As well as answering the inevitable queries ('Where's my overtime?'), the payroll department also has a busy time at the tax year end (5 April). It does not matter when the company ends its fiscal year, the tax year end is a set date. The payroll prepares and issues a number of forms at this time:

- **P60/P14** – copies are sent to the employee and the DSS of employee's earnings in that year. Earnings are shown after tax deductible items, such as pension contributions
- **P35** – this is a summary of tax/NIC due and paid by the company
- **P11D** – an employee earning more than £8,500 is deemed by the government to be a higher-paid employee! Such employees may be assessed for benefits in kind or non-cash payments, the most common of which is a company car. The benefits have to be listed on a P11D so that the tax authority can add them to its calculation of the employee's tax liability.

Cash book and petty cash

Receipts from customers and payments to suppliers, employees, government agencies – anyone – all have to be entered into the cash book.

Every so often, at least monthly, the cash book is reconciled to the bank statement. There can only be two reasons for differences and they have to be identified item by item to achieve a full reconciliation:

1 **Unlodged receipts** – these are cheques and cash paid into the bank but not yet showing on the statement
2 **Uncleared payments** – are cheques which have been issued but that have not been presented or that have not cleared the bank account.

For example, here are the last few entries in the company's cash book:

			Receipts	Payments
Balance b/f		£54,312.44		
23/7/06	Aspar Gmbh		£5,000.00	
23/7/06	Bugaboo		£2,750.00	
24/7/06	Chasthom		£1,550.25	
24/7/06	Aqua (1054)			£4,680.00
24/7/06	Efferedy (1055)			£812.15
			£9,300.25	£5,492.15
Balance c/f		£58,120.54		

The latest bank statement looks like this:

		Debit	Credit
Balance b/f	£54,312.44		
25/7/06 Payments in			£7,750.00
Balance c/f	£62,062.44		

The reconciliation is:

Balance per bank statement	£62,062.44
Plus unlodged receipts	£1,550.25
Less uncleared cheques	£5,492.15
Closing balance	£58,120.54

This leaves cash book and bank statement in perfect harmony.

It may be that unlodged receipts have not been banked yet or that it takes a couple of days for them to appear on the bank statement. The principles are the same when you balance your personal bank account – you do it by considering any cheques issued that haven't yet cleared and any receipts not yet showing on your bank statement.

One other duty is writing 'manual' or 'nominal' cheques. Mostly payments are made via cheque from a purchase ledger cheque run, but if, for one of a number of possible reasons, that is not suitable, then a manual cheque can be written. This literally means that someone writes out a cheque from the company cheque book and, like any other payment, it must be entered into the cash book.

Reasons for writing a manual cheque include:
• if a supplier refuses to wait until the next cheque run
• to pay organizations not set up on the purchase ledger (pension funds, employees)
• to reissue a cheque that has been stopped (perhaps due to loss in the post).

Company cheques, whether computer generated or hand written, usually require two signatures for security reasons.

Petty cash is a relatively small amount of cash kept on site for minor payments (milk bills, vending machines) and sometimes employee advances or expenses. All payments should be backed up by receipts and expenses claim forms and summarized weekly or monthly for posting to the general ledger to account for the expenditure.

The petty cash should be balanced at least monthly – the cash still in hand plus receipts and expense forms should equal the normal cash total.

The petty cash amount is reimbursed on the basis of what has been paid out (backed by receipts), usually by a cash withdrawal from the bank.

Fixed asset register

It also usually falls to Accounts to keep a list of all the company's fixed assets, in the form of a register. It can be either a manual record or a computerized one. The entry for each fixed asset will record the following details:
• asset reference no.
• description
• date of acquisition

- supplier
- original cost
- date of revaluation
- revaluation value
- depreciation period (years)
- accumulated depreciation
- net book value
- date of disposal
- proceeds from disposal

The accumulated depreciation amount is added to with each passing accounting period, with a corresponding reduction in the net book value (original cost less accumulated depreciation).

It is the sum of these records which goes to form the figures in the fixed assets section of the company's balance sheet.

The general ledger

The most prominent function of the Accounts department – the one thing that everyone knows they do, even if they know nothing else about Accounts – is that they are the ones who produce the financial results.

The key to the financial and management information reporting is the general ledger. As well as producing the reports, the Accounts department must also 'maintain' it through journals, accruals/prepayments, reconciliation of control accounts and by creating new account codes to enable more accurate reporting.

Other activities

One of the advantages of accounting is that it requires involvement with all other departments, since these, between them, originate the causes of all transactions. This often gives the Accounts department an insight into the workings of other areas, that surprises their colleagues. Hence accountants are usually represented on project teams, not just for their financial knowledge, but because they have a wider view and some understanding of the activities of other departments.

The Accounts department also produces cash flow forecasts, is heavily involved with budgeting and financial planning, perhaps even strategic planning. Any request for management information is normally directed at Accounts in the first instance and it is quite common for the head of the Finance department also to be responsible for the company's computer systems.

All in all, there are quite varied activities going on in the Accounts department.

Manual or computerized accounts?

Putting accounts on computer has given accountants the ability to process transactions much quicker and to recall them swiftly. However, computerized accounts are still based on the fundamental principles of double entry bookkeeping.

A key advantage of computerized systems is that the accounts can be integrated with other systems, e.g. stock control, payroll, sales order processing, purchasing and manufacturing. If information in one 'module' is passed through to another 'module', the whole package of software is referred to as fully integrated.

Modules from the same software supplier tend to have this advantage. However, modules from different suppliers can be made to 'interface' with each other if time, effort and money on programming are expended. If the modules are written in different computer languages, the task is made more difficult.

An easy way to overcome interface problems to the general ledger is to take the output from one system, e.g. payroll, and write out a journal using that output data.

Manual accounts, hand written into ledger books (readily available from all good stationers), are perfectly fine for small businesses, they just take a little longer to complete.

Key points

The primary daily activities of the Accounts department include:
- sales ledger
- purchase ledger
- payroll
- cash book
- petty cash
- general ledger
- financial reporting.

Other responsibilities may include:
- financial planning
- computing
- ad hoc project involvement.

Cash and profit

Much earlier, the distinction between cash and profit was made. The critically important role of cash flow management usually falls to the lot of the Accounts department, and is the next topic.

Chapter 18 Review Questions

1 What are the three main activities in the sales ledger area?
2 What would a statement of account tell your customer?
3 What would a supplier's remittance advice tell you?
4 In payroll, what causes the difference between gross and net pay?
5 How do the tax authorities know if a higher-paid employee receives benefits in kind?
6 What items cause the difference between the closing cash book figure and the bank statement balance?
7 What does 'fully integrated modular software' imply?
8 How can information be passed to the general ledger if there is no direct interface from another system?

19

cash flow management

Practical management of the cash flow

Controlling the cash flow on a day-to-day basis is usually the responsibility of the financial director or the financial controller. The principles for doing it well are quite simple (see below).

Money in comes from:
- debtors – which are determined by the level of sales and the credit terms given
- loans/share issues – which don't happen that often and then only when something big is brewing. This is not a daily concern for management.

Money goes out to:
- creditors – set by how much is spent on stock and overheads, labour, fixed assets and the credit terms received
- statutory bodies – Inland Revenue, HM Customs and Excise (VAT)
- employees – as their wages
- lenders/shareholders – in the form of interest, loan repayments and dividends.

There are two simple rules which are easier to state than follow. But, if adhered to, the rules will inevitably produce a growing pile of cash ready to spend in large amounts on fixed assets:

1 Sales revenues must be higher than all costs, which implies the company is in profit.
2 Goods and services must not be paid for until payment is received from the customer. This demands the co-operation of the supplier – imagine a nursery growing plants from seeds and cuttings. Until the plants have grown to a saleable size, then been sold and paid for, the company won't want to pay for the seeds. This could be months later.

An operating cash flow forecast, for use by management, is more specifically related to real cash than the additions and subtractions of the formal Cash Flow Statement:

Cash forecast for April

Week number	21	22	23	24
Receipts:	£375,000	£212,000	£374,000	£240,000
Payments:	£	£	£	£
Wages/salaries	12,000	12,000	12,000	40,000
NIC/PAYE			20,000	
VAT	280,000			

Direct debits		5,000	2,000	6,000
Creditors	112,000	84,000	220,000	65,000
Total payments	404,000	101,000	254,000	111,000
Movement	(29,000)	111,000	120,000	129,000
Opening balance	82,000	53,000	164,000	284,000
Closing balance	53,000	164,000	284,000	413,000

The receipts from customers will be forecast by Credit Control using the sales ledger to estimate due payments. In this example, the payments to be made in week 21 surpass the collections, reducing the bank balance. The company (i.e. the manager responsible) might prefer to try to delay some of those payments until it receives money due to it later in the month, to maintain a safe balance at the bank.

Controlling working capital

Keeping firm control of the company's working capital has an enormously beneficial effect on the cash flow, and vice versa. The key to doing this comes from looking after the elements of working capital and managing them properly – it does not happen by itself.

Stocks

- Keep stocks as low as possible (not buying stocks means not having creditors to be paid)
  BUT
- Beware of being overstocked, while avoiding stock outs and losing sales.

Debtors

- Have good credit control (see below).
- Remember that a sale is not a sale until it is paid for.
- Don't sell to anyone who won't pay!
- Keep customers to the terms.
- Shorter credit terms entitle you to get paid sooner.
- 'Early settlement' discounts may induce some customers to pay earlier than due, but they pay less for doing so.
- Get the paperwork right – invoice details must be correct to avoid delays in payment.

- Ask for payment! Make contact a couple of days before it is due to make sure there are no problems.
- Speak to the person who has the authority to arrange payment, not a clerk who can only pass the message on.

Creditors

- Get good terms – longer terms mean you don't have to pay until later.
- Try to arrange payment so that it follows receipts from customers.
- Do not abuse suppliers by making them act as a bank – what action do you take when your customers try to do the same thing to you?
- Prioritize payments if funds are limited (e.g. wages!).
- If purchases can be reduced, deferred or avoided, payment can be delayed or may not be required at all.

Credit control – getting the money in

The first task of Credit Control when faced with a potential customer is to establish a credit limit. This is usually done in conjunction with Sales which, in the normal scheme of things, would like a high credit limit to avoid lost sales. Ever cautious, Accounts will probably suggest a lower figure, wary of exposing the company to a potential bad debt (a customer who doesn't pay).

The credit limit can be based on a combination of trade references, bank references, a credit agency reference, Companies House reports (e.g. the latest statutory accounts), previous trading experience and the sales rep's personal knowledge of the company.

Once the account is up and running, Credit Control will monitor the customer's payment record. If invoices become overdue and persistent phone calls are not leading to payment, stronger action may be required.

Legal action can be threatened and enforced. In the meantime, the customer will be placed on stop, meaning that no further deliveries will be allowed. This often upsets Sales people who may be worried about offending the customer. Whether the account is reopened after payment has been made will be the subject of more debate between Accounts and Sales!

Factoring

One of the ways of improving cash flow is to factor debts. When this happens, the sale is made to the customer in the normal way. Then a factoring company pays the company immediately, usually about 80% of the invoice value. It has in fact 'bought' the debt.

The customer then pays the factoring company the invoice value, which passes it on to the supplier, less the 80% already advanced and its own fee, typically 5% to 10%. This can be an expensive way of doing business, but it does guarantee a swift income of cash after sales.

Credit insurance

Credit insurance is a way of insuring customers' debts, so that if a customer ceases to trade (i.e. goes bust), you can claim a percentage of the outstanding debt from the insurance company. Naturally, insurers don't like to cover companies which could go under, hence their scrutiny of the published accounts!

Like all insurance, there is a price to pay – but it's useful if you need it.

Key points

- Cash flow management is a vital activity. Companies can be brought down by a lack of cash rather than an absence of profit.
- In the daily life of a company, money comes in from debtors and goes out to suppliers, employees and statutory bodies.
- Credit control is the art of selling to people who are likely to pay and then getting the money from them.
- Controlling the elements of working capital – stock, debtors and creditors – enhances good cash flow management.
- Factoring is a costly way of securing swift payment on sales. Credit insurance can be taken out to reduce the risk of losses from bad debts.

Looking ahead

Accountants often get involved with the financial planning of the company. A discussion of the range and depth of the planning in which the company might indulge follows in the next chapter.

Chapter 19 Review Questions

1 What is the primary source of the daily receipts of cash in a company?

2 How does the management of the elements of working capital affect cash flow?

3 Define factoring.

4 What are the pros and cons of credit insurance?

20

corporate
financial
planning

In this chapter you will lear
- about strategic planning
- about strategic planning a
  the budget
- how budgets are used

Failing to plan

There is an adage that 'failing to plan means planning to fail'. Successful companies do not amble along, suddenly finding themselves market leaders. The directors of these companies will have planned how this will have been achieved. Even though not all their ideas and strategies will have turned out in the way that they hoped or expected, at least they had some method in mind to achieve their goal.

The alternative to planning is to drift along aimlessly, reacting to whatever happens each day. Planning is a function that is often carried out with considerable assistance from the Accounts department, since they have access to much useful information.

Strategic planning

This takes a long-term view, typically five years ahead, Some companies go for ten years, but many of the assumptions about future market and operating conditions are subjective even at five years ahead, so beyond that the data becomes highly speculative.

There are many theories of strategic planning, but most contain the following or similar elements.

Mission statement – this sets out what the company is about, what it stands for and what its values are.

Corporate objectives – given the company's mission statement, what are its objectives? These are not just financial – although making a profit is often an objective, it is usually not the only one or even the primary one. Other areas for consideration should include markets (which ones? what position in each?), products (which ones?), stakeholders (what are their objectives?), social (including environmental) issues, technological factors and the personal objectives of the management.

Internal and external analysis – if you want to get to Edinburgh, you need to know whether you're starting from Ipswich or Carlisle. Similarly, if the board wants to get the company to a position where it will have met its objectives, it needs to know where the company is now. Current financial status comes from the latest accounts, market shares are available from information bureaux (if not the company's marketing department) and evaluation of other parts of the business can come from a traditional SWOT analysis – strengths, weaknesses, opportunities and threats. Consideration of the external environment (competitors, suppliers, markets etc.) allows the planning team to judge what might change in the future.

Strategies – after all the information is safely gathered, the hard part comes – working out how to get from the current position to the desired one. The strategies will drive the company forward to achieve the objectives and are usually broken down into functional areas – there will be strategies for marketing, production, sales, financial, personnel, R&D etc.

The forward-thinking planner will also realize that some of the assumptions made about the future will not come to pass, so she will have in place contingency strategies. These are needed in case something goes wrong. Such disaster planning may include having action plans ready to cope with the loss of a major customer, destruction of a manufacturing site, the resignation of key personnel or changes in legislation affecting sales or production. Hopefully, these emergency plans will never see the light of day but, if the worst does happen, the management know what to do immediately. They don't have to spend days considering their options while everything collapses around them.

Short-term goals – five year plans are all very well, but they are actually achieved a day at a time. Consequently, the long-term strategies need to be translated into short-term goals, directing lower levels of management to tasks which will, when aggregated over the five years, culminate in the successful achievement of the corporate objectives. Setting goals is also a good way of communicating to employees what the corporate objectives of the company are and how they can help achieve them. It won't be done without them!

Review and re-plan – the strategic planning exercise is an annual one, even though the plan itself covers five years. This is because circumstances will not have turned out exactly as planned, nor will the company's performance have been exactly on target. It might even have been better than expected, leading to an upgrade in the objectives. So a review is carried out and the plan is revised if necessary.

Let's just take a moment to distinguish the company's goal from those of its directors and managers. Although they are the people who establish the corporate objectives, they will have their own personal objectives that they wish to achieve. Hopefully, these can be attained through the efforts made to attain the corporate objectives, in which case everyone will be happy. If there is a conflict between corporate and personal goals, something will have to give.

The budget

The logical short-term translation of the strategic plan is the annual budget. Expressed in financial terms, it covers just a year. In theory, its achievement should keep the company on track to achieve its corporate objectives. The textbook term for this is 'goal congruence'.

There are a number of important features of the budgeting process.

Top down or bottom up – even though the budget should align with the five year plan, how is it actually set? If senior management decide on the numbers ('We decree sales this year will be £12.5m.'), this is a top-down approach. It is then left to sales managers to decide how this target will be achieved and which products and customers will make up that total.

Alternatively, if those who have to implement the budget are given the initiative to set their own and the figures are consolidated to a company total (subject to board approval), this is the bottom-up approach.

In practice, the first is usually favoured since it is quicker, comes naturally from the strategic plan and, since the directors bear ultimate responsibility, gives them the final say.

Advocates of the bottom-up method point to increased motivation due to participation by lower levels of management, who may also produce more realistic goals being nearer the cutting edge. However, there are accusations of bias, as managers may seek to give themselves budgets that are easy to achieve, fearful of the consequences of not doing so.

There is also the problem of reconciling a bottom-up budget with the long-term goals. A bottom-up approach may yield a total of £10m sales when the board expect £12.5m to keep in line with their five year strategic plan. It may require a number of reworkings to reach a compromise (or to find a way of making the £12.5m!).

Zero base approach – this is an alternative and imaginative way of budget setting. Instead of putting limits and conditions upon managers, this process gives them some leeway and asks questions such as:

- 'If the board wanted sales of £12m, how much would you need to spend on advertising? How many sales reps would you need and how much would you have to pay them?'
- 'To produce 400,000 units next year, how much material will you have to buy? At what cost? How many people would you need in each area of production?'

As its name suggests, this approach starts with only a few assumptions. It does not impose the condition that what we do now must be copied next year, but allows managers the creativity of developing new ways of reaching solutions.

Its chief disadvantage is that it is a slow process. It is much quicker to determine next year's costs by adding 5% to this year's to allow for inflation and by assuming that the underlying activities will remain unchanged.

On the other hand, zero base budgets require thought, research, preparation and the ability to challenge existing assumptions. All of which probably account for its limited use!

Use of budgets

Budgets can be interpreted and used in a number of ways:
- to control operations
- to motivate staff
- to plan.

Control

The principal use of budgets is as a control tool. Deviations from budget are reported back to management (this is feedback) and lead to corrective action. The most common use of budgets by managers is to control:

> 'Kelly, you're 4.8% over your costs for this month!'

It is the heavy handed use of budgets like this that puts the whole budgeting process in a bad light. Kelly remembers last year when the budgets come round again, and decides to pre-empt any problems by adding an extra 5% to his cost budget – just in case and to avoid any future unpleasantness. And so the function of the budget is undermined.

Yet control is an important function and budgets play a vital part in it. They provide the comparison of budget against actual and make any deviations obvious, allowing managers to take corrective action.

Motivation

Budgets can also be used to motivate staff – bonuses can be paid dependent upon performance relative to budget. The budget becomes a target to be achieved, possibly stretching the management to reach new goals.

Letting middle and junior managers be involved in setting the budgets they will have to work with can increase their motivation, if done properly. Refusing to discuss the budgets and merely imposing them at the start of the budget period can certainly decrease their levels of motivation too. An individual manager who has her actual results measured against that budget is more likely to feel that the budget is achievable if she had a hand in setting it in the first place.

It's easy for Kelly to say that he did not set the budget and, furthermore, no one consulted him about it – if they had done, he would have set more realistic targets than the ones he was given and he wouldn't have gone 4.8% over.

The key words here are *responsibility* and *participation*. Responsibility is allied with *authority*. It is possible for a manager to be given responsibility for a budget for a cost, but have no authority over expenditure incurred. That is not sound practice, but it does happen. It is important to identify where both authority and responsibility lie, and to try to match the budget responsibility accordingly.

Planning

The budget is a plan, part of the strategic one. It represents the one year plan consistent with the organization keeping on track to meet its longer-term objectives.

The budget is a formal plan. The budgeted Profit and Loss Account and the budgeted Balance Sheet show the financial position that the directors or shareholders would be happy for the organization to be in at the end of the budget period. Indeed, if the budget is a true plan, it is where they would *expect* the organization to be, all other things being equal.

In addition, if the organization has long-term (strategic) plans, the forthcoming year's activities should help towards achieving the objectives of those plans. It follows that the budget is the plan for that year to keep the organization aligned with its longer-term goals.

The budget is a worthwhile plan in its own right, independent of its necessary connection to the strategic plan. Planning is an essential function of management, who, after all, are there to lead the organization. If they do not know in which direction and how far they intend to take the organization, how will they know when they have reached where they want it to be? Perhaps more importantly, how will they be able to tell if they are not heading in the right direction?

A plan, in the form of the budget, is a benchmark against which activities in the short term can be translated into results including, but not only, financial ones.

It is difficult for one set of numbers to achieve multiple objectives, which is one reason why budgets come in for some criticism. What is a plan to one manager becomes a rigorous target in the eyes of another. Top management may view the budget as the planned actual performance of the company. To others, it contains impossible targets to be achieved or goals for others to achieve. For most, it will be the benchmark by which their actions are measured, assessed and, quite frequently, rewarded too.

One budget, therefore, attempts to fulfil a number of functions and this can give rise to conflict. The Finance director may consider it to be a plan and so commits capital expenditure of the basis of anticipated future cash flows. The Sales director may turn the sales part of the budget into targets for the sales force to reach. It is even likely that she will set the goals with the budget in mind during the budgeting process. The Production director monitors his maintenance budget costs, minimizing expenditure.

These multiple functions of the budget need not conflict, but they can do. The Sales director may feel that because of market forces, she needs to spend over the advertising budget to ensure sales are reached. In some companies, the reply will be 'It's not in the budget, so it can't be done.'

Spending more on advertising means the plan would not be followed precisely, but if she does not make the necessary expenditure above budget, targets will not be met and actual results will differ from the plan anyway.

Reality v. budget

Never forget that the budget is not reality. When the budget is set, it is usually between three to six months before the start of the financial year to which it relates. That means that half way through the year, the assumptions upon which the budget was based are a year out of date. All sorts of things could have happened which render the budget less meaningful – a competitor could have launched a new product, perhaps two major customers merged, currency movements may have forced up the price of material imports.

It is important to realize that the budget may be wrong in such circumstances and that the slavish addiction to it may lead to short-term gain but a poor performance in the long term. To achieve this month's budget, costs may be cut and sales achieved through give away prices, but these successes in the short term may have a disadvantageous effect in the following months or years.

Forecasts

Once the budget for the year is set, it is usually set in stone, and it is the first point of comparison for the actual results. But because environmental operating circumstances do change, enlightened companies also have interim forecasts – mini-budgets which are more up to date. These can actually be enhancements of the original budget and come in the form of:

- rolling budgets – these just keep adding on another three months to the end of the budget, so there is always a plan for the next twelve months ahead
- flexed budgets – for instance, if sales are 10% up against budget, other elements of the budget are 'flexed' in line with the increase, to give a reappraised budget in line with a driving figure
- straight forecasts – another set of revised figures for comparison with actuals.

The Accounts department often prepares many of the financial figures in the budgets and forecasts, usually with the managers who will be responsible for seeing that they are achieved.

Cost centres v. profit centres

Centres, in this sense, are logical sections of the company which management wish to measure separately. They do not need to be physically separate, but often they are.

A cost centre is an area or department of the company that has its costs recorded in its own name. It often follows the departmental structure of the company, but may be more detailed than that. For instance, the Production department may be comprised of the following cost centres:
- goods inwards
- inspection
- assembly
- quality control.

Profit centres not only have costs set against them, but revenues too. It might be argued that inspection 'sells' passed materials to assembly and the more good product it passes, the more it 'sells'. In this way, management might seek to motivate individual areas to improve their profitability, in the hope that if they all do it, the overall profitability of the company would inevitably rise. The danger is that one profit centre may create profits at the expense of another, lowering the company's overall profit.

Profit centres are more usually encountered in situations where companies have different divisions, trading in different markets and products from each other, often physically separate too.

Key points
- Planning is an essential requirement for business success, although not a guarantee of it.
- Strategic planning takes a long-term view and looks at the 'big' picture of where the company wants to be, according to various measures and criteria, in five or ten years' time.
- Budgets are a more specific translation of the first year of the strategic plan and can also be used for control purposes, as well as motivating people. Setting the budget can be done by imposition from senior management or by aggregating the figures from the thoughts and opinions of lower levels of management.
- The budget has mixed and often conflicting uses – planning, controlling and motivating.
- Forecasts are the latest estimate of the company's likely achievements.
- Cost centres are concerned with the costs attached to an area of the company. Profit centres try to record the profit element generated by each area.

Your finances

Being able to understand the financial reports and activities of a company is useful knowledge to a manager from any background. Perhaps of more pressing interest is an understanding of personal finance, starting with the inevitable deductions of PAYE and NIC.

Chapter 20 Review Questions

1 What are the key elements of a strategic plan?
2 Why is external and internal analysis important in planning?
3 What are the three uses of a budget?
4 In which two ways can the numbers in the budget be established?
5 Define zero based budgeting.
6 How are cost and profit centres different from each other?

21

personal finance: income tax and national insurance

Making money and keeping it

The two traditional ways of making money are, first, to trade hours for pounds (working for someone else or yourself) and, then, invest spare cash to return more back. But whichever way you make it, the government is entitled to a share of your money, through taxation in one form or another.

Income tax

Working for someone else, and being paid by them, usually means that tax is deducted by the employer before you get paid under the PAYE (Pay As You Earn) scheme. Emoluments, the fancy name for earnings, are classed as Schedule E income.

There is a mathematical method for working out the tax liability after any given week or month during the year and at the tax year end itself. The end of the tax year is always 5 April.

There are two components to the calculation of tax – income and your personal tax coding. The coding itself has two elements to it, allowances and deductions.

1 **Allowances** – everyone starts with the a personal allowance.

Changes to these allowances are normally announced in the Chancellor's Budget. Generally the personal allowance can be expected to rise with inflation.

There are other allowances determined by the government – age allowances, disability allowances, etc. Your local tax office is a mine of information for these and all tax related matters, with leaflets to cover every subject.

Pension payments by the individual are also deductible for tax payments. In a company pension scheme, contributions will already be taken into account when the PAYE income tax is calculated. For those with a personal pension, the payments are made net of tax at the basic rate, so a higher rate taxpayer can have his tax coding adjusted to reflect the extra deductible contributions. This also applies to AVCs (Additional Voluntary Contributions).

There are other allowances, such as Gift Aid (single donations to charity) and charitable covenants. These allow the charities to claim back the basic tax and higher rate tax payers to reduce their liability. Again, the tax office provides full information on these and all other allowances.

Accountants (and other professional people) are entitled to tax relief on the subscriptions to their professional organizations if they need to be members to maintain their professional status.

2 **Deductions** – these reduce the tax coding, leading to more tax being paid. The most common are for benefits in kind received by employees – payments in a form that is not cash. This will include company cars, fuel for private use paid for by the company, beneficial loans (at interest rates lower than commercially available ones), private medical insurance and subscriptions to golf clubs, amongst other imaginative ways of rewarding employees without actually giving them cash.

It does not take into account the employer's contribution to the pension scheme on behalf of the employee.

The net difference between the allowances and the deductions is the tax coding. The last digit is replaced with a letter:

 L – single person's allowance
 H – married couple's allowance
 BR – no allowances, all pay is taxed at 25%
 T – there are taxable benefits
 NT – no tax deducted.

There are others, but these are the main ones.

Oddly enough, the letter is replaced by a 9 when the tax liability is calculated.

Those individuals unfortunate to have more deductions than allowances will have a negative coding, signified by a K. In this case, the tax code amount will be *added* to the earnings.

Week 1/month 1 basis

Normally the tax due is calculated on a cumulative basis, i.e. using the year-to-date figures rather than the ones in the particular pay period. It would usually work out the same anyway, unless the employee is paid in such a way that he crosses into a different tax bracket in any given period.

If the coding is signalled as a week 1/month 1 basis, then the tax is worked out on a period basis, not on the year to date. This tends to arise when the tax coding has changed significantly during the tax year for some reason.

An example – Joe Mendez

At the end of the tax year, Joe has earned £16,000 from his job as a bakery manager with Breadline Ltd. How much of that is overtime or bonuses is irrelevant.

Joe is married, his wife Ellen looks after their three young daughters full time. He pays 5% of his salary into the company pension scheme, which is matched by an equal payment from the company. He also receives free medical insurance for himself and his family, which costs the company £500 per year.

The tax allowances change every year at the whim of the government. In 2001/02, the basic tax allowance is the Personal allowance of £4,535.

This will show on Joe's tax coding, as will his deductions:

Benefit in kind	£500

This gives rise to a tax coding of £4,035, shown as 403T.

The current tax bands are (2001/02):

Taxable pay	Rate
£0–1,880	10%
£1,881–29,400	22%
£29,401+	40%

Joe's tax liability is worked out like this:

Earnings	£16,000	
Less:		
Pension contribution	(£800)	(5%)
Tax allowance	(£4,035)	
Taxable income	£11,165	
Tax due:		
£1,800 @ 10%	£180.00	
£9,365 @ 22%	£2,060.30	
Total tax due	£2,240.30	

Note that the pension contribution made by Joe's company does not affect Joe's tax liability. This means that it can be more effective to have the company pay more into Joe's pension than to give him a pay rise. He could even offer to swap part of his salary in return for the increased contribution, an idea known as a 'salary sacrifice'.

Joe is likely to have paid his tax of £2,240.30 during the year as his employer deducts income tax under PAYE. If he has paid more than that, he is entitled to a refund from the Inland

Revenue. Less than that and he owes them. However, if the amount is relatively small, they may simply deduct it from his next year's coding and recover it that way or, if he is lucky, forget it all together.

Another example – Georgina Jones

Georgina is a civil engineer earning £42,000 a year, with a company car which has a taxable benefit of £5,400. She is in the company pension scheme, paying 3% of her earnings. In addition she contributes £200 per month as AVCs.

Using the same assumptions as the previous example, her tax allowances are:

Personal allowance	£4,535

Her deductions:

Benefit in kind – car	£5,400

This gives rise to tax coding of –£865 (86K).

Using the same tax bands as before, Georgina's tax liability is:

	£
Earnings	42,000
Less:	
Pension contribution	(1,260) (3%)
AVCs	(2,400)
Add back tax allowance	865
Taxable income	39,205
Tax due:	
£1,800 @ 10%	180.00
£27,600 @ 22%	6,072.00
£9,805 @ 40%	3,922.00
Total tax due	10,174.00

Georgina can check on either her final payslip in the tax year or on the P60 she receives from the company, how much tax has been deducted from her pay during the year. Any difference to the above figure should mean a payment to or a refund from the Inland Revenue.

Tax avoidance v. tax evasion

It is perfectly legal to minimize the tax to be paid. Make sure that you are claiming all the allowances you are entitled to and, if you are a higher rate tax payer, that any tax deductible payments made net of the basic rate are included in your year end return to get relief at the higher rate (where applicable). So, tax avoidance is quite legitimate, even common sense.

What is not acceptable is tax evasion, such as failing to declare earnings and benefits in kind. This is punishable by law, with fines or even imprisonment, should the deed be discovered. Since employers declare such items on the P11D forms sent to the Inland Revenue, they will already know about them!

Year end forms

The year end tax return form asks for details of earnings, plus income from other sources (rents, bank interest etc.) and circumstances giving rise to allowances.

Employers give a P60 to their employees at the year end, detailing the taxable income to be declared on the year end tax return. This is already net of any contributions to the pension scheme.

Not everyone receives a year end tax return, usually just those receiving benefits in kind. Since the employers also send another form to the Inland Revenue, P11D, which shows benefits in kind, the Inland Revenue has a ready check on the individual's own return.

Optional self-assessment has been introduced allowing individuals to work out their own tax liability, as in the previous examples.

National insurance

As far as the individual notices, this is another direct tax on income. The rate varies depending on whether the individual is employed or self-employed, how much is earned, and whether he or she is in a 'contracted-out rebate salary related scheme'. Details, as ever, are available from the tax office.

Employers also pay national insurance, relative to the earnings of the employee, but there is no upper limit as there is for employees. The company also has to pay NIC on some forms of benefit in kind, including company cars.

Being self-employed

The rules are generally the same for the self-employed, the distinctions being that earnings are classed as Schedule A emoluments and payment of the tax is in two instalments, since there is no employer to collect it on a regular basis. The calculation of the tax due is the same as for an employed person, with allowances and deductions to derive a tax code.

Tax calculations

For those self-employed individuals who receive a tax form, they have the option of working out their own tax liability. The calculation can still be left to the Inland Revenue if preferred.

Keeping up to date

You can find the latest rates and allowances for the various taxes, as well as national insurance, on the Internet at www.inlandrevenue.gov.uk/rates.

Key points
- Income tax is a tax on gross pay adjusted by a person's tax code and permitted taxable deductions, such as pension contributions.
- Payments made to employees in a form other than cash may still be taxable as benefits in kind.
- Tax avoidance is simply arranging your financial affairs to minimize tax liability. Tax evasion is the illegal underpayment of due tax, usually caused by the under-declaration of income.
- National insurance contributions are another direct tax, with no scope for manipulation, although it does have a maximum amount payable.

Using money to make money

So that's how the government gets you to part with some of your money, although it has other ways too. With what's left, you can either spend it or put it to work to try and make more money – by investing it.

Chapter 21 Review Questions

1 What are the two components of an individual's tax coding?
2 What does a tax code of 240T imply?
3 What does a 'month 1' tax basis mean?
4 Differentiate between tax evasion and avoidance.

22

personal finance: investment

In this chapter you will lear

- how to use money to mak
  money
- about risk and reward on
  stock market
- about other investment
  options

Risk and reward

There is a story in which a newcomer asks an experienced investor, 'How do you make a small fortune on the Stock Market?'

The answer? 'Start with a large one.'

There are no guarantees of easy money to be had. If there were, we'd all be doing it! If you want to invest for higher rewards, there are inevitably higher risks – which may result in losing all the initial investment.

Which is, of course, why banks and building societies offer low rates of interest, because they are fairly safe homes for your money. Who ever heard of a bank going bust? Well, not many of them anyway!

Towards the other end of the risk scale, there are potentially large gains to be made in guessing which way foreign currencies will move and by how much. Get it right and you could be quids in – get it wrong . . .

First considerations

The chance to make millions playing the Stock Market may seem exciting, but there are some humdrum details regarding your personal circumstances that should be attended to first. There are other priorities for your money that should not be neglected, including, in no special order:
- life assurance (in case of death, leading to loss of income)
- pension (provision for your retirement)
- reducing borrowings
- permanent health insurance
- wills and inheritance tax planning
- personal financial requirements, e.g. holidays, a new car, school fees.

Not all of these may be applicable to you, but remember you can't top up a pension if you've got all your spare cash in a ten-year savings bond.

The effect of inflation

If interest on an investment is 4% p.a. and inflation is 6%, then the purchasing power of the investment is falling at 2% p.a. To show 'real' growth, an investment must return more than the rate of inflation. This can be either as income or capital growth.

Income from investing is returned in the form of interest and dividends. Capital growth is when the value of the investment rises (e.g. share values). Some investments offer only one, others both.

It is possible to swap capital for income, in the form of an annuity. Indeed, pension funds work this way, but it can be done with any lump sum of cash. The idea is that you have a large amount of cash which you are prepared to give to someone. In return, they will give you back an annual or monthly income of an agreed amount. The amount will depend upon numerous factors, such as the size of the lump sum, how old you are, and how long you are likely to live. These people do not want to pay out forever!

Safer options

There are lots of ways to make (and lose) money. The following are relatively safe, so have a relatively low return on the money invested.

Banks and building societies

Higher rates of interest are available if money can be locked up for, say, 90 days as opposed to being deposited in an instant access account. Switching from one institution or account to another is fairly easy – you know how much you're going to get (at least until the rates change) and access to your funds can be quick and simple. Non-taxpayers should be aware to register as such with the bank to avoid having tax deducted automatically from the interest.

ISAs

Individual Savings Accounts have the added benefit of paying the interest tax free. The disadvantage is that the money is tied up for five years and there may be penalty costs associated with switching to an ISA offering higher interest. Depending on how the money is invested, ISAs can carry some element of risk. A Cash ISA is like a bank deposit; but a Stocks and Shares ISA carries the risk inherent in Stock Market investment (see below).

There are government-set limits as to how much can be invested in an ISA in any given year.

National Savings

These come in various forms. Certificates and Index-linked certificates offer a guaranteed tax-free return if held for five years. Income Bonds pay gross interest which is subject to tax. Capital Bonds need to be held for five years for the full benefit, which is again taxable. Premium Bonds (the ones ERNIE picks) do not guarantee any return but the original investment is untouched. Minimum and maximum investment rules apply, further information available from leaflets in Post Offices.

Gilts

These are effectively loans to the government, so are viewed as being as safe as anything. There is a wide choice available, with maturity dates varying from within five years, five to fifteen years or no maturity date at all. On the maturity date, the loan is repaid. The price of gilts can change, reflecting the market (which is the sum of all investors) opinion of the relative positions of interest rates and inflation in the future.

Are any of these 100% safe? BICC went bust in 1990, although it appeared to be offering some high interest rates to attract funds. So did Barings (1994) after some losses in derivative dealings (see below). In theory, even the government could go bust – it's all a matter of relative risk.

A little riskier

The Stock Market

Also known as the stock exchange, this is simply a market place where shares in companies are traded. Buyers and sellers do not meet directly, but make their transactions through brokers.

Direct equity investment

This is simply buying and selling in shares of selected companies. Although the instructions to buy and sell are relayed through a broker, you can select the shares for yourself or have the broker manage your shares for you. He will be the judge of when and what to buy or sell.

The first is called an execution only service, which is cheaper, but you forgo the specialist knowledge the broker may have. Of course you may know better yourself!

The gains from direct equity investment come from dividends paid out by the company (so many pence per share) and the rise in the share price. For example:

January – buy 10,000 shares in Dolphin plc at 40p each =	£4,000
June – dividend payment of 2p/share =	£200
December – shares now valued at 48p each =	£4,800

The potential gain is £800, although this is not realized until the shares are sold. Add to this the dividend received and the notional profit in the year is £1,000. For an investment of £4,000, that represents a return of 25%.

Of course, as they say in the small print, the value of shares can go down as well as up.

Since profit made when shares are sold is subject to Capital Gains Tax (CGT), there is a technique called 'Bed and Breakfasting' which may reduce the liability to CGT. Since each individual has an annual allowance for CGT of £7,500 (in 2001/02), it may be sensible to sell the shares at the end of the tax year and buy them back at the start of the next tax year. There will be a transaction cost for doing so, but if the profit made on the sale is less than £6,000 (assuming no other capital gains made elsewhere), then there is no CGT to pay.

The commonly used ratios relating to share prices have been covered in Chapter 7, such as earnings per share, price/earnings and dividend yields.

Another term worthy of note is *cum-div* (or *ex-div*), which means that you can buy the share *with* its next dividend payment (or *without* it).

Unit trusts

Since you would need a lot of money to invest in the shares of, say, fifty separate companies to spread the risk, a more accessible way has been developed. These are unit trusts, which themselves purchase the shares in the companies. They use the funds from all the investors in the unit trusts.

This means that an individual investor does not own shares in Marks & Spencers, but they may have 600 units of a trust that does. It will also have shares in many other companies.

The unit trust is a sort of middle man which allows investors with relatively small amounts of money to spread the risk of their investments. Units can be bought by a lump sum or by periodic payment. The investments made by a trust can be sector or country specific, or quite general (UK, North American, Pacific Basin, equities, fixed interest, index linked, cash etc.).

Investment trusts

An investment trust is actually a company which is itself quoted on the Stock Exchange, although its only business is investment in other companies' shares. The value of its shares depends upon the investors' perception of the management's abilities to invest wisely. There are a number of other technical distinctions between investment and unit trusts. It tends to be seen as slightly riskier than a unit trust, but with the potential for higher returns (and bigger losses!).

Derivatives

This is getting towards the scary end of risk, sometimes charitably described as 'informed speculation'. The danger is that you have to think you know something that everyone else doesn't – like what the dollar exchange rate will be in 6 months time. But some people do, and get it right. Others get it wrong!

There are two distinct types of derivatives available to the individual investor, futures and options, neither of which have to involve shares in quoted companies. The investment can be used to buy currencies and commodities (metals, coffee, pork bellies!) which are transacted in an open market.

1 **Futures** – are agreements to buy or sell something on a specific date at a specific price. A futures contract might stipulate that I will buy 1,000 tonnes of lead at £350/tonne on 14 February.

Now it is unlikely that I will want to take delivery of the lead in February – what I would be hoping for is that the price of lead will be more than £350/tonne on that date, so I can sell it immediately and make a profit, e.g. if the price is £370, the profit is £20 × 1,000 = £20,000.

If it isn't at least £350, I will make a loss – I will have to sell the lead straight back to the market at the prevailing price, say £300, losing £50 × 1,000 = £50,000 (unless I can find somewhere to store 1,000 tonnes of lead and I have the £350,000 required to pay for it!)

Futures can only be traded through stock market institutions.

2 **Options** – are similar to futures, but you don't have to go through with the deal if the prices haven't come out in your favour. For the privilege of being able to duck out of it, you pay a premium for the contract upfront. A *put option* allows the buyer of the option contract to sell the asset at a future date at a specific price. A *call option* allows you to buy it in the future at a certain price.

This can be done with shares. Note that with a put option, to sell something in the future, you don't even have to own it now. The intention is that you will buy it (at the current price) just before you sell it (at the option price).

If I have a put option on 2,000 Sainsbury shares on 4 November at £2.50 each, I will exercise it if the shares are valued at less than £2.50 on that day. Say they are at £2.44:

Buy 2,000 shares at £2.44 (via my broker) = £4,880
Exercise the put option – sell at £2.50   = £5,000
Gain   £120

If the shares were more than £2.50, I would just let the option lapse, although I would have lost the initial premium. It may be that the premium is less than the gain made anyway, but it would reduce the loss.

Very risky investments with potentially very high gains

At the far end of the scale, you could dabble in antiques, art, coins, stamps, comics – whatever there is a market for. There are no guarantees!

Consider the term

Most of the places to invest your money mentioned above are not ways of making a few quick bucks. They are generally regarded as medium- to long-term investments of five years and upwards. Share prices are not known for doubling overnight, although individual ones can show sudden and dramatic increases (or decreases) in the face of new information such as a take over bid (or a scandal).

Who are the investors?

Most shares in quoted companies are held by other institutions rather than private individuals. These include pension funds, using the contributions from their members (and their members' employers) to invest in other companies, with a view to being able to provide for the payments to be made to their retired members in the future.

Professional advice

So, there all these choices, but what is the best way to proceed? Financial advice is available, though never freely. A fee-based adviser will offer, as you would expect, advice in return for a fee. The alternative is to take recommendations from someone who is commission based – that is, he takes a cut from whatever investments and policies he sells to you. Some such advisers are tied to a single company and can only offer their products, others have a freer role in selecting their recommendations.

To protect the public, the rules and regulations concerning financial advisers are becoming increasingly strict. All advisers come under the watchful eye of the Financial Services Authority (FSA) (for more information, check its website at www.fsa.gov.uk).

However, be aware that authorization of these bodies is no indicator of ability, merely recognition of authority to transact.

Diversify

You've taken professional advice, you've conducted your own research into investment opportunities, what do you do next?

The sensible strategy is to build a portfolio of investments, starting with low risk ones (with low rewards), building up to medium risk and then topping them off with relatively higher risk ones – available funds permitting of course.

Similarly, if investing in the Stock Market, the prudent strategy is to spread the investment over a number of companies in different sectors, rather than risk everything in one company or in one industry. There are higher transaction costs, because there are more transactions, but the risk is diversified.

Key points

- There is a trade off between risk and reward. The higher the risk, the higher the potential rewards and losses.
- The safe end is represented by banks and building societies. Riskier are stock market investments, such as shares, unit and investment trusts. At the extremes come derivatives and tangible assets.
- The sensible strategy is to build a portfolio of investments starting with safer investments and building up to riskier funds as funds and preferences permit.
- Do bear in mind that some forms of investment are little more than a gamble and it is sage advice never to gamble with money you cannot afford to lose.

The government wants more

Having put your spare money to work in one form of investment or another, you still can't escape giving the tax man another share. There are even more taxes to be aware of than just income tax and national insurance.

Chapter 22 Review Questions

1 What is meant by the 'real' growth of an investment?
2 How does 'bed and breakfasting' reduce capital gains tax liability?
3 As the potential rewards of differing investment opportunities rise, what happens to the corresponding risk of losing everything?
4 In which two ways can a professional financial adviser earn remuneration?
5 What is the advantage of a diversified portfolio of investments?

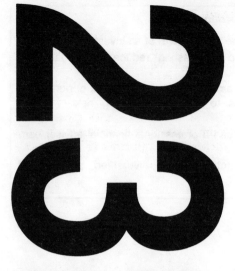

23

personal finance: capital gains tax and others

In this chapter you will lea

- about personal taxes
- about capital gains and other taxes
- about corporation tax ar the individual

Unearned income

The Inland Revenue distinguishes money made from investments as 'unearned income' and as such it is subject to capital gains tax (CGT). The most common way for this to arise is by selling shares at a higher price than was paid for them, this being the capital gain.

However, it can also apply, as in the examples given in the previous chapter, to the gain made on selling works of art, a second house (a main residence is exempt from CGT), horses – anything that is deemed to be a 'chattel'.

Allowances

The first £7,500 (in 2001/02) of capital gains is exempt from CGT.

If there are losses made on the disposal of capital items, these can usually be set off against any gains made, to leave the net chargeable gain which is then subject to CGT to the extent that it exceeds the £7,500 personal allowance.

Allowing for inflation

Because of the nature of capital items, they are generally held for a number of years. Given the impact of inflation, this means that the value of something would have to grow just to maintain its original worth. For instance, if shares in a company cost £10,000 when originally purchased, with inflation at 5%, you would need the shares to have risen in value to £10,500 after one year just to stay as valuable as they were.

The Inland Revenue recognizes this fact by allowing chargeable gains to be reduced by an inflation index that is published by them. The original purchase cost is inflated by the figure quoted which will reduce the gain, or perhaps even turn it into a loss!

The rate of tax due is calculated by adding the gains to the individual's taxable amount from earned income and will result in a rate of either 20% or 40%. For example:

In January, Zoe, a basic rate tax payer, buys 10,000 shares in Lemmings plc at £1.10 each – the published index is 224.6.

The following November she sells them at £2.22 each, when the index has reached 227.8.

Her capital gains tax liability is calculated as:

Proceeds from sale	£22,200
Cost of shares	£11,000
Gain	£11,200
Less index adjustment £11,200 × (224.6/227.8 = 0.9859)	
Adjusted gain	£11,043
Less personal allowance	£7,500
Taxable gain	£3,543
Tax due at 20%	£708.60

There are more taxes

Inheritance tax

The estate of the deceased, if it is not passed on to a spouse, is subject to inheritance tax to the extent to which it exceeds £242,000 (2001/02). The applicable rate is 40%.

This explains why the likes of the rich and famous (rich anyway) sometimes have to sell off family heirlooms to pay the tax man – houses, lands, art collections etc. are all calculated in the value of the estate, but the tax must be paid in cash and it can be quite a sizeable amount.

The way round inheritance tax is to give all your money away before you die! Ideally, you'd think you'd want to do that just before you passed on, but the Inland Revenue are too smart to be caught by that one. Gifts made to others during the seven years preceding death are added back in to determine the value of the estate and the tax liability. It seems there is no cheating either death or the Inland Revenue!

Value added tax

The standard rate of VAT is 17.5% and this is added to the cost of all supplies that are not zero-rated or exempt. In addition supplies of power and fuel for domestic or charity use are subject to VAT at 5%.

A business must register for VAT (and so add VAT to its invoices) if its turnover exceeds the registration limit (£54,000 for 2001/02). Only a business registered for VAT can claim back the VAT it pays on any invoices received from its suppliers. It follows that most businesses will charge and reclaim VAT, usually with a net charge to be paid to HM Customs and Excise:

VAT quarterly return for Abacus Ltd		
	£	£
Sales	800,000	
Output VAT		140,000
Purchases	620,000	
Input VAT		108,500
VAT payable		31,500

This example implies that all Abacus' sales and purchases attract the standard rate of VAT at 17.5%, although there are exempt and zero-rated supplies. It also suggests that a business making a profit will always owe VAT to the VAT authorities. This is usually the case, although a business could claim VAT back under the right circumstances, such as if its sales are exempt (e.g. exports), or it has made higher purchases than normal (more VAT to claim back) and the products are still in stock and therefore unsold (without the VAT charged to the customer).

The textbooks are fraught with legal cases struggling over precise definitions of taxable supply and whether they are zero-rated, exempt or chargeable.

The distinction between zero-rated and exempt is that zero-rated supplies must be included in the calculation to determine whether a business has exceeded the VAT registration limit. Such supplies include food, books, clothes and a host of other defined areas. However, it does mean that a business such as a bookshop can register for VAT, not charge VAT to its customers and reclaim the VAT on its expenditure.

Exempt supplies, on the other hand, are not considered for VAT purposes at all. These include businesses selling land, insurance, finance and others. Of course, if they carry out other trading activities which would be subject to VAT, the business can reclaim some of its VAT (known as having partial exemption).

Corporation tax

Naturally this only applies to companies. Sole traders and partnerships – the self-employed – are not companies and their earnings are assessed under income tax.

It is a complicated subject for which professional advisers charge large fees. However, the main points are as follows:

- The statutory accounts are not the same as the tax accounts. Some types of expenses are not allowed to be deducted for tax purposes, such as entertainment of customers. Strictly speaking, the only expenses allowed are those incurred wholly and exclusively for the purposes of trade.
- Depreciation is replaced by capital allowances, which broadly allows 25% of the cost of plant and machinery additions to be deducted, e.g. a machine bought for £20,000 and depreciated over ten years gives rise to an annual depreciation charge of £2,000. For corporation tax purposes the capital allowance is £5,000 p.a. for the first four years only.

In reality, it is much more complicated.

A company with taxable profits over £1,500,000 pays tax at 30% (2001/02). There are rules to work it out for points below.

Key points

- Two more personal taxes are capital gains tax and inheritance tax, both having scope to reduce the amount of tax paid through good planning.
- Value added tax is an indirect tax, added to many items purchased daily by business and the general public. Suitably registered organizations can claim back VAT; the public must grin and bear it.
- Corporation tax is the business equivalent of income tax.

Chapter 23 Review Questions

1 To what sort of profits does capital gains tax apply?
2 How does indexing reduce the size of a capital gain?

appendices

A: UK accounting bodies

The UK is different from its European trading partners when it comes to having professionally qualified accountants. Firstly, there doesn't appear to be exactly the same thing anywhere else. Certainly, other countries have financial managers and bookkeepers, but there doesn't seem to be the same insistence on professionally examined qualifications. Experience counts more.

So, not only does the UK prefer to have its accountants qualified by examination, it goes overboard on policy and has different professional bodies for various types of accountants!

The Institute of Chartered Accountants in England and Wales

The ICAEW has a parallel organization in the Institute of Chartered Accountants in Scotland and there is another body for Ireland.

The members of these bodies, which are separate from each other, regard themselves as 'the profession'. By and large, these are the auditors and most of them do their training within the body. (The training is called 'articles', since auditors wish to be likened to that other august profession, the legal one.)

Once qualified, Chartered accountants either make a move into commercial business, stay in the audit field as a manager or specialize in one of the more diverse areas such as taxation or management consultancy, looking for eventual progression to a partnership.

The Association of Certified Accountants

Some members of the ACA are allowed to audit company results, if they have the right qualification from the ACA. Their members tend to work in commercial businesses, but it is possible to find them in auditing companies.

The Chartered Institute of Management Accountants

CIMA members are generally employed by commercial organizations and are not allowed to audit company accounts. They are usually the ones to prepare them.

These are the three sought after qualifications, although there are two other worthy bodies.

The Chartered Institute of Public Finance Accountants

CIPFA members come from government institutions such as local government and the NHS.

The Association of Accounting Technicians

This body is regarded as having a lower status of qualification than the others, as accreditation with it gains the holder partial exemption form the examination of the other bodies. It is a perfectly respectable qualification in its own right, probably much underestimated.

Membership of one body does not preclude joining another.

In practice there is little to distinguish the members of these various bodies. Historically there has been an intangible suggestion as to the relative value of each qualification, in the order given above. However, since all their students sit examinations on similar subjects, they are similarly knowledgeable and employment becomes a question of individual experience and ability.

In the 1980s and 1990s, there were talks between the various bodies with the aim of merging a number of them, eventually into a single organization representing all qualified accountants. There has been no success so far.

B: Legal structure of trading entities

In the eyes of the law, trading organizations can have a different legal status from each other. Sometimes the distinction between them isn't important. On other occasions, it can be absolutely critical that you are clear exactly which type you are dealing with. These are the most common forms of trading organizations.

Sole traders

This is when Joe Soap buys and sells on his own account. He is an individual, wheeling and dealing. He may have to be registered for VAT if his turnover crosses the registration limit, but his net income from his business operations is subject to income tax, not corporation tax.

He is responsible for his own debts and is sued in his own name if he defaults on payment to his creditors. All his other personal assets are at risk to settle any such claims.

Partnerships

If Joe and Mary trade together, they are partners. The rules of their partnership are decided between them – who is responsible for what and how the profits are to be shared. Each share of the profits from the business is declared on their own income tax returns.

Normally, they would be jointly and severally liable, in legal parlance, for the actions of each other. This applies however many partners there are. In practice it means that if Joe can't pay for something purchased in the name of the partnership, then Mary has to. Each is given authority to commit both of them to transactions on the partnership's behalf.

Any court case against them would be in their individual names, although it would probably refer to any trading name they had for their business. Again, their personal assets could be used to settle any claims against the partnership, no matter which partner instigated it.

Limited companies

A limited company must show the word 'limited' or its abbreviation 'ltd' (or 'plc') after its name and give its registered number on its letterhead. It is all right for Joe to trade as 'Joe Soap & Company', but this is not a limited liability company, merely a trading name.

The benefit of a limited company is that the most the owners can lose is their initial stake in the company. Company law recognizes that a company is a legal person and can make transactions in its own name, through its directors and managers. The liability of the shareholders for the debts of the company is limited to their equity investment.

A limited company must have at least one director and a company secretary. This latter is an officer of the company, not a typist! It must also have a registered office where it can be contacted. No one is a director of the company (no matter what their job title) unless such appointment has been registered with Companies House on form 288.

There are rules (now) to stop people setting up companies, buying lots of valuable things on credit and disappearing into the sunset, leaving an angry posse of creditors. These rules are by no means watertight, but people have been barred from being directors if they have a record of running unsuccessful companies.

So Joe and Mary are the directors and shareholders of Soap Suds Limited. Their personal assets are now protected from creditors, except in certain legal circumstances (i.e. if they continued to trade while the company was insolvent and was, therefore, technically unable to pay its bills). But in cases of disputed bills, or contract breaches, it is the company which is sued, not Joe and Mary. Or it is the company which brings legal action against others, not Joe and Mary.

The profits of the company are subject to corporation tax, which is generally higher than income tax. Of course, any remuneration Joe and Mary take out of the company in the form of salaries or dividends must form part of their own individual income for the year and is taxed accordingly. There is a price to pay for the protection of limited liability.

That price also includes the need to file accounts at Companies House every year, as well as other information such as the names and addresses of company directors. This information is publicly available, to competitors as well as suppliers.

Public limited companies

A plc is a public limited company which has the same rules as a limited company but, because its shares are publicly available on the stock market, it has to disclose more information. Or privately held limited companies reveal less, depending which way you look at it.

Plcs for short, these are the same as limited companies, only that the shares are for sale in the stock market. There are further regulations set by the stock market which apply to plcs, but for the purposes of the court, the company is still a legal person, protecting shareholders with the shield of limited liability.

So always know who you are dealing with – an individual or a company. If things go wrong, you might need to know who to sue.

C: Companies House details

Companies House holds the annual returns, accounts and mortgage registers of all limited companies. The accounts of a company must be sent to Companies House within nine months of the company's financial year end and most companies leave it as long as they can before doing so. There are over a million companies registered in Great Britain.

The annual return shows the directors' and shareholders' details and the mortgage register if there any mortgages over the assets of the company.

All this information is available from Companies House, at a fairly small charge.

There are several Companies Houses from where information is available, in Cardiff, London, Edinburgh, Birmingham, Manchester, Leeds and Glasgow. For general enquiries about the services available from Companies House, the number is Cardiff (01222) 380801.

They are also capable of producing other information, such as a list of the companies of which a particular individual may be a director.

D: Information for decision making

The Accounts department, in common with other departments, is a producer of information, in particular that with a financial bias. This includes such reports as the Profit and Loss Account, the Balance Sheet and the Cash Flow Statement. Generally information, financial or otherwise, should meet three criteria:

1 **Timely** – information must reach the recipients in time for them to be able to act upon it. It's no good reporting that the company has become overdrawn three months after it has happened or that the scrap rate was an excessive 10% four weeks ago.

2 **Accurate** – wrong information can be worse than no information, since it may lead to actions that make the situation worse. Also the information should be couched in appropriate terms – senior managers are happy to talk in round thousands or even tens of thousands of pounds, depending upon the size of the company. There is no point in spending time and effort in being accurate to the nearest pound when such detail is not required.

3 **Relevant** – there is no point in sending information to someone who cannot do anything about it. Why tell the warehouse manager that Bashers Ltd has gone over its credit limit? She can't do anything about it, but the sales manager or credit controller could.

That all said, the financial reports do have a special distinction in that they measure the organization in its attempts to meet its primary objective – profitability (or possibly to break even for non-profit seeking organizations). If the management of the company becomes aware (hopefully quite quickly) when profitability levels are not as high as required, more detailed analysis can provide the reasons why. The finance function, often in conjunction with the computer department, is usually the provider of most of the information used by management to run the company.

Some information can come directly from the responsible department, but usually anything with a monetary value is initiated, if not finally reported, by Accounts.

For example:

Sales department	*Production department*	*Accounts department*
Quantities		Revenues
	Quantities:	
	Production	Costs
	Stock	Values

It is apparent that teamwork is essential – Accounts cannot calculate stock values without accurate stock quantity data, supplied by Production or maintained by Production, on a computer system.

Information produced for its own sake is a waste of time, money and effort. So is giving the information to people whose decisions are not influenced or guided by it.

index

teach yourself ®

Afrikaans
Access 2002
Accounting, Basic
Alexander Technique
Algebra
Arabic
Arabic Script, Beginner's
Aromatherapy
Astronomy
Bach Flower Remedies
Bengali
Better Chess
Better Handwriting
Biology
Body Language
Book Keeping
Book Keeping & Accounting
Brazilian Portuguese
Bridge
Buddhism
Buddhism, 101 Key Ideas
Bulgarian
Business Studies
Business Studies, 101 Key Ideas
C++
Calculus
Calligraphy
Cantonese
Card Games
Catalan
Chemistry, 101 Key Ideas
Chess
Chi Kung
Chinese
Chinese, Beginner's

Chinese Language, Life & Culture
Chinese Script, Beginner's
Christianity
Classical Music
Copywriting
Counselling
Creative Writing
Crime Fiction
Croatian
Crystal Healing
Czech
Danish
Desktop Publishing
Digital Photography
Digital Video & PC Editing
Drawing
Dream Interpretation
Dutch
Dutch, Beginner's
Dutch Dictionary
Dutch Grammar
Eastern Philosophy
ECDL
E-Commerce
Economics, 101 Key Ideas
Electronics
English, American (EFL)
English as a Foreign Language
English, Correct
English Grammar
English Grammar (EFL)
English, Instant, for French Speakers
English, Instant, for German Speakers
English, Instant, for Italian Speakers
English, Instant, for Spanish Speakers

English for International Business
English Language, Life & Culture
English Verbs
English Vocabulary
Ethics
Excel 2002
Feng Shui
Film Making
Film Studies
Finance for non-Financial Managers
Finnish
Flexible Working
Flower Arranging
French
French, Beginner's
French Grammar
French Grammar, Quick Fix
French, Instant
French, Improve your
French Language, Life & Culture
French Starter Kit
French Verbs
French Vocabulary
Gaelic
Gaelic Dictionary
Gardening
Genetics
Geology
German
German, Beginner's
German Grammar
German Grammar, Quick Fix
German, Instant
German, Improve your
German Language, Life & Culture
German Verbs
German Vocabulary
Go
Golf
Greek
Greek, Ancient
Greek, Beginner's
Greek, Instant
Greek, New Testament
Greek Script, Beginner's
Guitar
Gulf Arabic
Hand Reflexology
Hebrew, Biblical
Herbal Medicine
Hieroglyphics
Hindi
Hindi, Beginner's
Hindi Script, Beginner's

Hinduism
History, 101 Key Ideas
How to Win at Horse Racing
How to Win at Poker
HTML Publishing on the WWW
Human Anatomy & Physiology
Hungarian
Icelandic
Indian Head Massage
Indonesian
Information Technology, 101 Key Ideas
Internet, The
Irish
Islam
Italian
Italian, Beginner's
Italian Grammar
Italian Grammar, Quick Fix
Italian, Instant
Italian, Improve your
Italian Language, Life & Culture
Italian Verbs
Italian Vocabulary
Japanese
Japanese, Beginner's
Japanese, Instant
Japanese Language, Life & Culture
Japanese Script, Beginner's
Java
Jewellery Making
Judaism
Korean
Latin
Latin American Spanish
Latin, Beginner's
Latin Dictionary
Latin Grammar
Letter Writing Skills
Linguistics
Linguistics, 101 Key Ideas
Literature, 101 Key Ideas
Mahjong
Managing Stress
Marketing
Massage
Mathematics
Mathematics, Basic
Media Studies
Meditation
Mosaics
Music Theory
Needlecraft
Negotiating
Nepali

Norwegian
Origami
Panjabi
Persian, Modern
Philosophy
Philosophy of Mind
Philosophy of Religion
Philosophy of Science
Philosophy, 101 Key Ideas
Photography
Photoshop
Physics
Piano
Planets
Planning Your Wedding
Polish
Politics
Portuguese
Portuguese, Beginner's
Portuguese Grammar
Portuguese, Instant
Portuguese Language, Life & Culture
Postmodernism
Pottery
Powerpoint 2002
Presenting for Professionals
Project Management
Psychology
Psychology, 101 Key Ideas
Psychology, Applied
Quark Xpress
Quilting
Recruitment
Reflexology
Reiki
Relaxation
Retaining Staff
Romanian
Russian
Russian, Beginner's
Russian Grammar
Russian, Instant
Russian Language, Life & Culture
Russian Script, Beginner's
Sanskrit
Screenwriting
Serbian
Setting up a Small Business
Shorthand, Pitman 2000
Sikhism
Spanish
Spanish, Beginner's
Spanish Grammar
Spanish Grammar, Quick Fix

Spanish, Instant
Spanish, Improve your
Spanish Language, Life & Culture
Spanish Starter Kit
Spanish Verbs
Spanish Vocabulary
Speaking on Special Occasions
Speed Reading
Statistical Research
Statistics
Swahili
Swahili Dictionary
Swedish
Tagalog
Tai Chi
Tantric Sex
Teaching English as a Foreign Language
Teaching English One to One
Teams and Team-Working
Thai
Time Management
Tracing your Family History
Travel Writing
Trigonometry
Turkish
Turkish, Beginner's
Typing
Ukrainian
Urdu
Urdu Script, Beginner's
Vietnamese
Volcanoes
Watercolour Painting
Weight Control through Diet and
  Exercise
Welsh
Welsh Dictionary
Welsh Language, Life & Culture
Wills and Probate
Wine Tasting
Winning at Job Interviews
Word 2002
World Faiths
Writing a Novel
Writing for Children
Writing Poetry
Xhosa
Yoga
Zen
Zulu

available from bookshops and on-line retailers

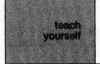

small business accounting
mike truman

- Are you new to small business?
- Have you tried and failed to understand traditional book keeping?
- Do you want a reliable way of controlling your finances?

Small Business Accounting provides practical guidance on how to keep the books and prepare the accounts for your small business. Forget about debits and credits, journal entries, ledgers and day books – if you can read a bank statement this book will teach you how to prepare accounts, make forecasts of your cash-flow and prepare a budget.

Mike Truman is a Chartered Accountant, a Fellow of the Chartered Institute of Taxation and a writer on accountancy and taxation.

teach
yourself

book keeping
andrew lymer & andrew piper

- Are you new to book keeping?
- Do you want to cover the basics then progress fast?
- Do you need to brush up your skills?

Book Keeping is a straightforward introduction to the principles of book keeping and the practical skills of recording transactions, posting the ledgers and preparing final accounts. It provides worked examples throughout, together with a wide range of carefully graded questions and exam papers with sample answers.

Andrew Lymer is a Senior Lecturer at the University of Birmingham, where **Andrew Piper** was an Honorary Research Fellow.

teach yourself

setting up a small business
vera hughes & david weller

- Are you setting up a small business?
- Do you need help to define your product or service?
- Are you looking for guidance in marketing and finance?

Setting Up a Small Business helps you with all the everyday aspects of running a small business and gives detailed guidance on specialized areas such as legal requirements, opening a retail or office-based business, staff selection and marketing.

Vera Hughes and **David Weller** started their own business in 1980, having been involved in the retail industry for many years. They have written a number of books on retailing.